AFTER THE STORM

After the Storm

by
Col. E. H. Jim Ammerman (Ret.)
and
Rev. Charlene Ammerman
with
Andrew Collins

Star Song
COMMUNICATIONS
Nashville, Tennessee

Star Song Publishing Group, a division of
  Jubilee Communications, Inc.
2325 Crestmoor, Nashville, Tennessee 37215.
Printed in the United States of America.

First Printing, April 1991

Library of Congress Cataloging-in-Publication Data

Ammerman, E. H. Jim.

    After the Storm / by E. H. Jim Ammerman and Charlene
Ammerman with Andrew Collins.—1st ed.
    p.   cm.
    ISBN 1-56233-023-3
    1. Persian Gulf War, 1991—Religious aspects.
2. Chaplains, Military—United States.   3. Chaplains,
Military—Persian Gulf Region.   4. Persian Gulf
War, 1991—Veterans—United States.   I. Ammerman,
Charlene.   II. Collins, Andrew, 1953–   III. Title.
956.704′3—dc20   91–13253
                                                         CIP

98 97 96 95 94 93 92 91 — 8 7 6 5 4 3 2 1

After the Storm is dedicated to . . .

All the God-fearing, caring chaplains who served our Lord Jesus Christ and the U.S. Military in Desert Shield and Storm.

Jim and Charlene Ammerman

The late Dr. John E. Douglas, Sr., a man of God who gave the whole of his life and energies to feeding the hungry, reaching the lost, and spreading the Good News of Jesus Christ all around the world.

Andrew Collins

A Proclamation by President George Bush

AS THE PSALMIST WROTE, "O GIVE THANKS TO THE Lord for he is gracious, for His mercy endures forever." Almighty God has answered the prayers of millions of people with the liberation of Kuwait and the end of offensive operations in the Persian Gulf region. As we prepare to welcome home our courageous service men and women and join in the joyful celebrations of the Kuwaiti people, it is fitting that we give thanks to our Heavenly Father, our help and shield, for His mercy and protection.

Asking Him to judge not our worthiness but our need and protection, and knowing that the Lord gives victory "not by might, nor by power" we prayed for a swift and decisive victory and for the safety of our troops. Clearly, the United States and our coalition partners have been blessed with both. We thank the Lord for his favor, and we are profoundly grateful for the relatively low number of allied casualties, a fact described by the commanding general as "miraculous." Nevertheless, because each and every human life is precious, because the massive scale of Operation Desert Storm must never diminish the loss of even one service member, we also remember and pray for all those who made the ultimate sacrifice in this conflict. May the Lord welcome all who have fallen into the glory of Heaven, and may He strengthen and console their families in their hour of need. May it also please our Heavenly Father to grant a full recovery to those military personnel wounded in action.

We also give thanks for the remarkable unity of our people throughout this conflict—a unity marked by heartfelt and generous support for our troops in the field and, in the American tradition, respect for the rights of those who dissent. May our Nation emerge from this conflict stronger and more united, to face as one united people the challenges and opportunities before us.

As we unite in thanksgiving to Almighty God, let us pray in a special way for the innocent men, women, and children—wherever they may be—who have suffered as a result of the conflict in the Gulf. Recalling the words of President Wilson shortly after World War I, let us seek forgiveness for any "errors of act or purpose" and pray for God's help and guidance on the way that lies ahead. May the resolution of remaining questions and concerns, especially the return of all prisoners of war and the freeing of those who are detained, be as timely and as certain as this victory in battle.

Finally, seeing before us the promise of a safer, more peaceful world—one marked by respect for the rule of law—let us offer all these entreaties in a spirit of faith, humility, and gratitude, seeking reconciliation with all people. In so doing, we recall the timeless prayer found in Scripture:

> Thine, O Lord, is the greatness, and the power, and the glory . . . for all that is in heaven and in the earth is Thine . . . and Thou reignest over all . . . in Thine hand is power and might; and in Thine hand it is to make great, and to give strength unto all. Now therefore, our God, we thank Thee and praise Thy glorious Name.

As the Psalmist wrote, "Come behold the works of the Lord . . . He makes wars to cease to the end of the earth."

Contents

Foreword

THE MEDIA DUBBED IT THE "ONE HUNDRED-HOUR War." To those of us at home, the battle between Iraq and the Allied Forces (spelled A-M-E-R-I-C-A-N) was a "Living Room War"—brought to us courtesy of Cable News Network (CNN). It was, they said, a tribute to America's military might and technical superiority.

For one, it was a war of uniques.

But if this is all we saw of the war, we missed the real victory.

For the first time in many years our president came on national TV with but one challenge to the American people. He asked us to pray. Later, after the war was over, that same president issued a proclamation designating three days as "National Days of Thanksgiving." He called on the American people to:

- ". . . give thanks to our Heavenly Father, our help and shield, for his mercy and protection.
- ". . . thank the Lord for His favor, and the relatively low number of allied casualties.
- ". . . pray for the innocent men, women, and children—wherever they may be—who have suffered as a result of the conflict in the Gulf.

- ". . . seek forgiveness for any errors or act or purpose and pray for God's help and guidance on the way that lies ahead.
- ". . . gather in homes and places of worship to give thanks to Almighty God for the liberation of Kuwait, for the blessings of peace and liberty, for our troops, our families, and our Nation."

At the same time, in an unprecedented move, Jerusalem's chief rabbi, during Purim, the holiday commemorating Queen Esther's victory over Haman (spelled S-A-D-D-A-M-H-U-S-S-E-I-N), prayed that all members of the alliance would be blessed and that there would be peace. It was a remarkable prayer. He called on all Jews to bless their traditional enemies—Syria and Saudi Arabia—who were part of the coalition.

All these things were the result, not of American military superiority and technical brilliance, but of the hand of God at work before and during the war.

The day before the war broke out, Chaplain (Col.) Jim Ammerman spoke in our church in Melbourne, Florida. A career military officer, he did not speak of our military prowess. Rather he told of the remarkable revival that was taking place in the Saudi Arabian desert. He told of the thousands of young Americans who had committed their lives to Jesus Christ. This was significant, for it was before the shooting began, meaning these were not proverbial "foxhole conversions."

He told of the Bibles that had been distributed to American troops—and were being given away to the other coalition troops, including many Muslims. He told of the crammed chapel services, the spontaneous Bible studies, the water baptisms in the desert, and the metal crosses the men insisted they be allowed to wear with their dogtags.

He also spoke of the more than 70,000 caskets that had been ordered by the Pentagon—just in case.

It was a powerful moment as our church, along with churches around the world, joined in prayer for quick victory and safety of our loved ones.

President Bush called it a "just war." Some question if a war, any war, can ever be just. The aim of this book is not to convince you one way or another. The aim of this book is to tell you about the other "forces" at work in the war other than the military forces. These were the invisible forces at work in the Heavenlies—which miraculously took form in the desert.

Jim Ammerman is more than my good friend. He is one of a very few mortals to break through where even angels feared to tread, and pioneer in new spiritual areas among men of war.

Jamie Buckingham
Palm Bay, Florida

Introduction

WAR IS BAD. THERE HAS NEVER BEEN A "GOOD" WAR because, by definition, war means battles fought and men killed as people aren't able to solve their differences through peaceful means. The cost of war is undeniably terrible—but, as improbable as it sounds, good things often come from war.

I hate war. It is evil, a deadly and very destructive evil. Having served in World War II, Korea, and Vietnam—having seen the death and destruction that took place in these killing fields—how could I hate anything more than I hate war? Could there be anything worse? As a matter of record, yes.

Tyranny is worse than war. How many of us would want to live under a tyrant like Saddam Hussein? Anarchy is also worse than war. Who would want to live in a society where everyone decides what he wants to do and can do—and gives no thought for other people? Who would want to live in a land without law or reason? And enslavement is worse than war. It is far better to die fighting for freedom than to spend life in the chains of repression and forced service.

Yet at what price should a war be waged? When is it time to take up arms and fight for a cause? At what point is there no other way to resolve a situation? What cause is great enough to consider taking another man's life or giving up your own?

Desert Storm was fought over oil—at least that is what we have been led to believe by most members of the press. Is that the whole story? And if it is, is oil—so vital to the American economy—enough of a reason to take up arms?

In actuality, Saddam Hussein invaded Kuwait because he wanted to rule the world. His dream of controlling all people and all nations may not have been much different than that of earlier kings or dictators except in scope. Certainly his vision was different from Hitler's, but his goals were the same. Saddam seemed to see himself as the Nebuchadnezzar of the 1990s. Before he died in 562 B.C., Nebuchadnezzar had ruled the entire world as he knew it, and it was in his footsteps that Saddam wanted to follow. He had spent millions in an attempt to restore the glory of ancient Babylon, and now he wanted OPEC to help him hold the free world hostage through an oil price hike. When he couldn't get his way in closed-door meetings with fellow OPEC nations, Saddam decided on a more aggressive plan of action—he took over Kuwait. Next in line was Saudi Arabia. If he could control Saudi and combine its resources with Kuwait's huge oil reserves, then he would be the major dealer in world energy and the keeper of the world's purse strings. He would have economic control over every major nation in the world. And who knows what devious methods he would use to ensure his continued power?

With his mind set on world domination through

economic means, Saddam would have become a modern Nebuchadnezzar. He would have even controlled the United States. Our very freedom and way of life would have been at the mercy of his decisions about oil prices and quotas. Desert Storm was not fought over oil, but over freedom!

Even with this background information in mind—even knowing what might have happened given the right amount of time for Saddam to act and enough apathy on the part of the world community—was it worth going to war? Did anything good really come from it?

First of all, by sending our brave men and women to the Persian Gulf to stop Saddam, we probably saved thousands of their lives. How? If these 540,000 Americans had not gone to war, if they had instead stayed home and driven U.S. highways for those seven months, two to three times as many would have died. Is that a miracle? Yes, that is a miracle on a grand scale. This war actually saved the lives of many of our young people. Imagine that! But more good came from the war than even these spared lives.

I believe one reason why so little blood was spilled, so few lives lost, and even so many lives saved was because America went to God in prayer before we went to war. We prayed by the millions. We prayed with heartfelt sincerity and tears of supplication. We asked God for a miracle, and we received it. In fact, we received not just one miracle, but countless miracles during both Desert Shield and Desert Storm.

As was widely reported in the news, the projected worst-case scenario was that one-half of America's aircraft would be lost in the first week of the Gulf War. We lost six planes. Our nation's leaders came on TV and radio news programs telling us not to be too optimistic—the worst was still to come. Yet they seemed to be talking more to themselves than to the public. They just couldn't believe how good the news from the Gulf really was, and they were preparing us for what they believed had to come later. They didn't understand why more of Iraq's anti-aircraft fire wasn't hitting the allied targets. Even lucky shots should have been able to knock down more than just six planes. So why wasn't it happening?

The military knew, you knew, and I knew that we had the best in high-technology planes and weapons. We also had well-trained pilots who were flying at their highest level of alertness and concentration. Thanks to the Arabs, none of our men had access to alcohol, drugs, or nightly carousing. For the first time in aviation history, we were all flying sober and alert. Yet even that fact couldn't have been responsible for such a dramatically low death toll. So what was it?

God had entered the scene of world events just as He had in the days of Nebuchadnezzar and Babylon. The Lord God Jehovah was moving on behalf of His praying people. He has always been this kind of Lord, He is today, and He always will be.

Experts outlining the worst case scenario for a land war projected that at least seventy thousand

American men and women would die. Can you imagine that many caskets coming home? The War Department was so sure of this number that new mortuary facilities were added to already large centers at Pope Air Force Base in Dover, Delaware and Fort Bragg, North Carolina. Cemeteries in Saudi Arabia, complete with pre-dug graves numbering in the tens of thousands, were prepared for men and women who would die as a result of their exposure to toxic gas. These American soldiers would have had to stay in the desert forever. The chemical warfare would have kept them from ever returning home. The U.S. government could not have exposed its citizens to the toxins that had infected and killed these thousands. We just knew these losses had to happen!

Ah, but God moved again. As you will read in this book, a freak wind change—a once-in-a-lifetime shift that lasted throughout the Gulf's normally windy season—took away the effectiveness of Saddam's most terrible weapons. Who knows how many innocent lives—on both sides of the battle lines—were saved as a result?

We had encouraged people to pray that just seven thousand of our land forces—ten percent of the projected loss—would have to give their lives for this cause, and our people prayed earnestly. Did God answer our prayers? We asked for a miracle. Did He respond? Deaths in the Persian Gulf War came to one-tenth of one percent of what we had prayed for: seventy people lost their lives in a war in which more than seventy thousand had been expected to die. The caskets were not needed, and neither were the enlarged morgues. God had listened to a humble people, and He had responded. He had spared life after life after life. This was a miracle on a grand scale, and you need to stop right now—don't read any farther—and thank Him for those whom He allowed and is allowing to come home!

Statistics are convincing, and knowing that men and women were saved on the battlefront—and actually saved by being on the battlefront—is deeply moving, but this information addresses only the physical well-being of our men and women. What of their spiritual well-being? That is another story entirely, and that is why we have written this book. The spiritual dimension of what happened in the Gulf is, I believe, the reason why this war started a worldwide revival that will see more conversions of new Christians than we have ever known!

When our troops in the deserts of Saudi faced their own mortality and when all of us waiting at home were reminded of our own mortality, we all looked to God. Like the sailor who came to our chaplain's cabin door at 2:00 a.m. and tearfully admitted, "I can't sleep—I'm afraid to die!," many of us opened our eyes to the reality that life is indeed fragile. The sailor listened carefully as our chaplain told him about Jesus, and, a few minutes after sharing his fears, he left that cabin a saved man. He knew the Lord as his personal Savior, and he knew that he had a heavenly home, an eternal dwelling place in heaven.

At about this same time, a young soldier surrendered his heart to Jesus while he was alone in his desert tent. He was so overwhelmed and filled with joy that he ran around and around the tent, crying and praising God. In the middle of Saudi Arabia, a new Christian was alive in the spirit and knowledge of Jesus Christ!

When our comfortable routines and our daily habits are disrupted by something like the deployment of men and women to the Gulf region, we experience a certain openness to new things. This openness led to many dramatic changes in the very fabric of people's souls. In Saudi, the usual escapes of alcohol, drugs, and adultery—things often used to mask our need for Christ and His love—were gone. But Jesus was there! Praise God that tens of thousands of our soldiers, sailors, Marines, and Air Force personnel came to know Him in the Gulf. Multitudes more were restored to an earlier faith and commitment to Him!

Our chaplains' reports were filled with exciting testimonies about how God's Spirit was at work in the Gulf. Day after day, they reported, men and women were surrendering their lives and hearts to Jesus. Some of the most hopelessly lost were the first to turn to Christ.

This duty in the Persian Gulf was the most fulfilling ministry that most of our people had ever known. So many people were baptized in "Canvas Cathedrals" that congregations seemed to double in size every time they held services. With so many men and women being saved, and so much accomplished for the Lord, our chaplains felt a new vigor and enriched spiritual growth. They were personally blessed by the presence of the Lord. Superlatives abounded in their letters, telephone calls, and relayed messages.

We had encouraged our Full Gospel Chaplains to have everyone who made a decision for Christ write home at once about their new life and spirit. This act confirmed within the individual and for all of those close to that person that he or she really knew the Lord. It was an important first step in sharing and witnessing, and it was also a first blessing!

On the home front, the family members and friends who received the good news of their loved one's salvation could celebrate with them. If, by chance, the people receiving the news were not Christians, then they too were forced to consider the condition of their own soul. And if the soldier who was saved was one of the seventy who didn't make it back home, at least the letter confirmed that he or she had found an eternal home with God. Those left behind in this life didn't have to worry about the loved one's soul being lost forever.

Of course, the sharing of the Good News is the foundation for the really wonderful result of this war—a revival that will sweep the decade. And this revival needs you!

God has not forgotten America, and it became obvious during the Gulf War that millions of Americans have not forgotten God. What is He doing in your life? What is He saying to you as an individual and to us as a nation? And where is He leading our great land? To know Jesus, to follow Him as Lord and

Savior, and to live an abundant life is the motivation of many Americans today. And God has called those of us who are following Him to action and revival. Let us face this challenge and the future with energy and great expectancy.

Praise the Lord! Good things do come out of war!

Col. E. H. Jim Ammerman (Ret.)
Director of the Chaplaincy
Full Gospel Churches

CHAPTER ONE

A Christian Holy War

"We swear . . . that we will make the gulf a graveyard for all those who think of committing aggression, starting with those cowardly American navies."

Baghdad Radio—August 1990

NEVER IN HISTORY HAD THE WORLD CHANGED SO quickly. The preceding two years had seen massive political upheaval in Russia, the dissolution of the Warsaw Pact, the emergence of democratic governments in former bastions of communism, and the willingness of once-atheistic governments to open their borders to Christian missionaries. Churches closed by government decrees decades before were now opened by those same ruling bodies. The world was changing rapidly. These truly were unique moments in modern history.

The Cold War was declared over, and the West had supposedly won. And while problems still existed on a huge scale, Christians had been invited to preach and teach behind what was once the iron curtain. There was a chance for worldwide revival, a chance to share with millions a message that can fill empty souls and give purpose to people's lives, and yet to a large degree Christians—individual believers as well as Christian organizations—held back. We American Christians were witnessing a miracle, but we seemed to view it more as an illusion than a godly gift.

So, it should have come as little surprise when, like a thief in the darkness, Saddam Hussein threw down his sword as a challenge. Under the cover of an August night, his elite Republican Guard rolled into Kuwait. Within hours, the Iraqi army controlled the country, and Saddam claimed as his own one of the richest oil-producing nations in the world. Like a child climbing a hill and pushing smaller children down the side, he dared anyone to dispute his right to play international games by his own rules.

A desire for money and a ruler's personal ambition lay behind Iraq's invasion. Saddam wanted to replenish a treasury depleted by an eight-year conflict with Iran and a multi-million dollar restoration of Babylon. Only then could he hope to build up his war machine. But more than money, Saddam needed an easy and well-publicized victory to restore his image of invincibility for his Arab neighbors and himself. The long Persian Gulf War between Iran and Iraq had left neither side a winner and both countries much poorer. It had been a war of viciousness and cruelty taken to extremes not practiced since World War II. Interestingly, during the confrontation, most of the world supported Saddam's regime.

In retrospect it is easy to find fault with supporting—for any length of time—a man who has used poison gas on his own people, but for years the United States, Britain, France, and even Russia had given advice and supplied hardware for Saddam's cause. The world's fear of Iran had laid the groundwork for this fanatical and unprincipled dictator's quick rise to his position as one of the most powerful forces in the Middle East. In some Arab circles, Saddam was viewed as a real hero.

The United States, however, regarded Saddam as cruel and vindictive, a politician to be supported only because he was better than the alternative. "Demonic" was a word often used to describe this man, so how could people call this vile individual a hero, look up to him, and even name their children after him? The answer lay in something that few Americans knew—Arab history. Just as the fall of communism in the Eastern Bloc had opened the door for Christian revival there, the history of the Gulf region had served a madman's rise to power and was now presenting another opportunity for Christian evangelism.

Although civilization in the Middle East is nearly six thousand years old, none of the countries in the region have existed for much more than seven decades, and some gained their identity less than fifty years ago. This area has long been dominated by outsiders. Consequently, millions of people have for centuries looked for a leader of courage and direction to take charge, someone to rally behind, someone to lead them. They hoped for an Arab George Washington.

Until 1918, the Middle East was under the strict control of the Ottoman-Turkish Empire. This confederation was successor to the great Islamic empires that had ruled the area for more than thirteen hundred years. In World War I, the Turks lost control of the area, and, under the mandate system, the Persian Gulf was seized by the French and British. For both France and Great Britain, this was a last-ditch effort to maintain their influence in international politics and commerce.

The British and the French essentially carved out the countries which we know today. Their goal was simple: to keep the Arab world in a state of disunity and therefore easier to control. The Europeans didn't consider the area's historical background or the cultural ramifications of their actions; they simply acted in their own interests. They were, for instance, vague about who really owned what. Even today the borders of most countries are in question, resulting in constant strife and ongoing disputes.

Much of what the free world knows of the Arab people dates from the time of European occupation. The romance of the French Foreign Legion, the dashing flare of such men as Lawrence of Arabia, and the romance of ancient rulers and buried treasures were played out time and time again in literature and on film. Yet the reality of this distant land was far different.

The reality behind this false Western image was a people who resented foreign control and domination, and this resentment dated back to the invasion of the Middle East by the Christian crusaders in the eleventh, twelfth, and thirteenth centuries. With the control of their governments, their people, and their resources in the hands of men who knew nothing of their culture or religion, the people's discontentment grew more and more intense.

After World War II, the British and French gave up what was left of their Arab empires, and the United States moved in to keep the U.S.S.R. from gaining control. During this period, the nations of the Middle East seemed to be more under the control of oil companies than their own governments. What foreign oil companies wanted, foreign oil companies got. Under this system, rulers became rich, the haves became powerful, and the vast numbers of have-nots became even more disgruntled. They desperately prayed for a leader who would take charge, someone who would free them from what they viewed as the greedy Christian influences overtaking their world.

When Arab lands were set aside for the new nation of Israel, the people's frustration reached its height. The Palestine Liberation Organization and other groups rose up and used terror as a tool to gain control of the region. The United States, the one nation which fully supported and underwrote the Jewish state and therefore was seen as Israel's closest ally, was at the top of the enemy list, and Christians—who embraced the Jewish people and basically ignored the Palestinians—were regarded with even greater contempt. Over the next ten years, an Arab self-awareness was born. Suddenly, rather than waiting for a sign from heaven, a new generation was ready to fight to unify the region.

The first active strike against the "Christian infidels" came from Iran. Since most Arab people had little use for this nation, this was not a significant moral victory for most. The Arabs regarded the Iranians as Persians, invaders from another time, and did not consider them true members of their race. When Saddam stood up to the foreign invaders, he polarized a frustrated people ready to take action. Saddam was the common person's hope for a united Islamic nation that would span the Gulf region. He would drive out the Christian influence, the corrupt rich leaders, and the oil companies, and he would destroy Israel.

The rulers of the major Arab states, however, viewed Saddam with great suspicion. Politically, he was dangerous—he just might be able to unite enough Palestinians to bring civil war to a number of regions. With his huge army, his high-tech weapons, an air force that was one of the world's largest, and a fanatical desire for power, he might be able to stir up the people enough to destabilize the area, upset the local and world economies, and ultimately unite the region under his rule. Because of his great popular appeal, the neighboring rulers couldn't topple him. Instead, they tried to appease him, and for years they managed—until Saddam entered Kuwait. There, the Arab leaders drew the line.

Earlier, Saddam had wanted Kuwait to support an oil price-hike that would help his country rebuild its treasury, depleted by the war with Iran. When

Kuwait resisted, Saddam met with his advisers and military leaders. Most pleaded that he be patient: a confrontation which would likely involve the United States and alienate a now free-thinking Moscow hardly seemed worth the risk.

Saddam listened to the dissenters and then shot more than one hundred of those who disagreed with him. After replacing them with men he could trust and who would support him, Saddam invaded Kuwait. As a shocked world watched on Cable News Network (CNN), the United States received calls from most of the other Arab states. The leaders in the area were almost all in agreement: "We have to act, but we need your help." Even though few people recognized it at the time, the Lord was opening another door for sharing the hope of the Gospel.

In the United States there was debate, there was disagreement, and there was open discussion, but mostly there was worry. Hundreds of Americans in Kuwait were being rounded up and held as hostages and human shields. Saddam was waving them like a red flag in front of a bull. He was determined to show up America's weakness by using captured American civilians to motivate our surrender to him. Yet, rather than divide us and force us to capitulate to his demands, Saddam's actions had the opposite effect. For the first time in the latter half of this century, the people of the United States stood together, one in their conviction and emotions. We were not going to tolerate this violation of human rights from a man who seemed to have as little regard for life as Adolf Hitler.

While Saddam bragged, President Bush mobilized the troops and asked a nation to pray. Within weeks, United Nations sanctions were in place, and American forces in the region numbered close to 100,000. Saddam, still sneering and issuing random threats, was branded an outlaw. As he spoke of holy battles to come, Americans lined up behind their leadership and prayed for the Allied forces.

On the home front, the sacrifices had begun. An already-faltering economy had been further shaken by uncertainty about future energy supplies and prices. Gas prices had climbed, and some businesses had seen layoffs. With more and more troops needed for duty in the Gulf, reservists were leaving jobs and families in ever-increasing numbers.

A host of military experts wrote articles and gave speeches on the cost of a Gulf War. They shook their heads at the prospects of bringing Saddam under control. Many of these thinkers said that anyone believing that this operation wasn't going to take years and cost hundreds of thousands of lives, probably believed in miracles.

Yet, much more than at any time in recent history, believing was becoming a way of life. While it was true that few Americans knew or understood the Gulf and its history, it was also true that Saddam had underestimated the strength, conviction, and spirit of the American people. Although Vietnam may have sapped us of our patriotism and pride in our military, and even though Germany and Japan had dealt major blows to our economy, few Americans were ready to admit that our nation's best days were behind us. Deep down inside we still needed to cry out when we saw moral injustice, we still desired to lead the fight for right, and we still had the urge to openly wave our flag and pray to God for His blessings on our country and peace in His world.

Saddam's dangerous miscalculation was to judge Americans as weak-kneed, soft-spined has-beens who would submit to a bully. He was banking on us having learned from Korea and Vietnam the high costs and few rewards of being involved in international affairs. Saddam believed that we would back down or, at worst, compromise with him and that, when we did so, he would be one step closer to ruling the entire Gulf. With the world's oil under his control, he felt he could rule the world.

Within months, though, Saddam faced an overpowering enemy. One in every 480 Americans was in the Persian Gulf as a part of the international coalition allied against Saddam, and they were all there to right a wrong. For the first time in decades, Americans were involved in a moral battle, a fight that was worthy of our convictions, a war that would lead us not only to victory but also to a restored zeal for the flag and for the Lord.

Saddam declared the war a "holy" one, but the United States would be the nation to experience the revival. Beginning in small churches in rural America and dusty tents on the Saudi plains, this revival spread across the nation and throughout the war theater. The invasion of a country with fewer than two million people had ignited a spark that could spread the flame of Christian influence across the country and around the world by the end of this century. What the fall of Communism in Eastern Europe couldn't do, what thousands of sermons had failed to do, and what tens of thousands of books and magazine articles had not done, Saddam had managed to accomplish in one night: his actions had initiated a rebirth of faith. Christians suddenly found that their spirits had been renewed.

The time was right, the people were ready, and the world's ears were open, and in the middle of the Islamic nation of Kuwait, a Christian holy war began. This was the start of the most far-reaching mass revival in modern times.

CHAPTER TWO

Are We Ready?

"It was for such a time as this that God called me into the chaplaincy."

A Desert Storm Chaplain—November 1990

WHEN SADDAM INVADED KUWAIT, HE SET IN MOTION events that he couldn't have foreseen. He had no idea that the United States would stand firm, nor could he have known that the people of our nation would overwhelmingly support their leadership. He also couldn't have guessed the reaction of the rest of the world, especially his Arab neighbors and our international allies, who lined up in support of the U.S. position. But more than any of this, he never could have imagined that the invasion of such a small nation would trigger a huge back-to-the-Gospel movement in both the military and the civilian populations of America.

Preparedness has become a watchword in recent times. In magazine articles, newspaper editorials, television broadcasts, radio reports, and presidential press conferences, the term has come up over and over again: "Are we prepared to take on Iraq? Are our forces prepared to join in a war that will be unlike anything we have ever experienced? Will our high-tech weapons actually be able to hit their targets—and are the men and women who control them prepared to use them? What is the state of our preparedness?"

The word *preparedness* has been chiefly associated with the military, but it is a term that surely could, and probably should, apply to personal Christian faith: Are we prepared to face death and are we equipped to meet it? Are we prepared to witness to the lost? Are we prepared to live a life that testifies to our faith and exemplifies Christ's love? Are we prepared to pray with power and conviction? What is the state of our Christian preparedness?

Chaplains have been involved in helping people answer questions like these for almost as long as we have been sending soldiers into war. In naval aviation during World War II, I attempted to prepare men to face their Master. I witnessed to, read Scripture with, and prayed alongside hundreds of young men who were later lost in missions against the enemy. I know the ache of loss as well as the agony of questioning whether a sailor had accepted the Lord before he answered his last call. I knew firsthand that, in many cases, giving a life for a country also meant losing a soul to the devil.

In Korea and again in Vietnam I served my nation as a chaplain. During these strange conflicts—these wars that were fought not with the idea of winning, but with the goal of holding the enemy in check—I served with the U.S. Army. Again I talked with men who were facing death, and again I asked them to look into their hearts and turn their lives over to Jesus.

After Vietnam I was stationed in Frankfurt, Germany, with the V Corps. There I supervised eighty-three chaplains from fourteen different denominations who ministered to fifty thousand troops and their dependents. It was far different from my experience on the battlefield, but it was a job that began to open my eyes to the way that many chaplains performed their duties. I was distressed to see that some chaplains simply went through the paces. They didn't have a zeal or fire for the Lord, and they didn't seem interested in knowing whether their flocks were in a state of preparedness, much less helping them get there. For these men, the chaplaincy wasn't a calling; it was merely a job. The more I witnessed this kind of chaplain, the more concerned I became about the future of our service personnel and the overall chaplaincy program.

Early one morning in February of 1974, I was skiing alone on a mountain in Berchtesgarden, Germany. It was a beautiful day with rich blue skies, soft white snow, and sunshine bright enough to enlighten any man's mind. With all of the Lord's handiwork so richly displayed, how could I not feel close to the Creator? As I propelled myself down the slopes, I began to pray—not the kind of prayer where you bring before God the concerns of your heart, but one where you open your mind and allow God to speak. I wasn't expecting to receive much more than a renewed sense of purpose as I raced down the mountain, but somewhere on the middle of the slope I heard a voice.

"I will make you the head of the chaplaincy."

The voice was clear, yet when I looked around, I saw no one. I then realized that the Lord had visited me. He had actually reached out and directly touched me in a way that I had never before experienced. Stunned, I thought about His words. Rather than clearing my mind, the statement I had heard raised a host of unanswered questions.

Another man had already been assigned Chief of Army Chaplains for that period of time. So how could I be made the head? When I returned to the hotel, I told my wife what had happened. When neither of us could find the answers to my many questions, I retired to a place by myself and spent the day in prayer. The answers did not come immediately . . . .

From Europe, I was transferred to Fort Leavenworth, Kansas, where I was the post chaplain and pastor to the Command and General Staff College. There I worked with over one thousand of the most promising mid-career officer students in the service, men who were training to be our country's next colonels and generals. While I found the work rewarding, I couldn't help thinking back to the words I had heard on that snow-covered German mountain. Was this really where I was supposed to be? Was this what God had in mind for me?

When I retired from the Army in 1977, I had served my country as a chaplain for over twenty-three years, finishing my career as a colonel. I had worked alongside such respected career brass as the brilliant General William Westmoreland, and I had gotten to know green draftees who had little or no knowledge of matters of war. I thought I had seen it all, and I thought that my duty was complete; that, as far as the military was concerned, I had exhausted my usefulness for the Lord. Yet in the back of my mind was that haunting statement, "I will make you the head of the chaplaincy."

Upon ending my service to Uncle Sam, I was eager and ready to pastor men, women, and children among the civilian ranks. Not only did I have more than two decades of active duty to draw from, I was also a product of the best schooling a minister could claim. I had earned a Doctor of Theology and received a Doctor of Divinity. I had been an ordained minister since 1946 and a Spirit-filled Christian since 1938. I knew that I could do the job that was ahead of me, and yet I wondered if I was leaving something unfinished behind in the military.

In 1981 I was pastor of the Beverly Hills Baptist Church in Dallas, Texas. I was involved in many different aspects of the church's ministry, including weekly national radio and TV broadcasts. I was respected by my peers and my congregation. My career as a preacher was alive, growing, and vital, but still I felt as if I was supposed to be involved in something even greater. It seemed to me that the Lord had prepared me and called me to something very special, something much different from what I was doing, and I knew that I had to seek what it was He wanted for me. With that gnawing awareness in my heart and mind, I gave up my pulpit and spent fourteen months in prayer.

In June of 1983, it suddenly became clear to me

that a huge segment of the United States population was not represented in the chaplaincy ranks of the military. Full Gospel Churches were growing and thriving in a country that had seen the influence of its major denominations wane, yet these same independent churches were not represented in the armed forces. Their men and women were not being served, and other nonbelievers were not being touched by their enthusiasm for the Lord. "Why," I asked myself, "should the most vitally alive group of Christians in America not be allowed to exert its life-giving influence in our armed forces?" I then set about using my lifetime of experience and my wealth of military connections to change the system for the good of God and the country.

It took thirteen months for the Chaplaincy of Full Gospel Churches to meet the requirements and receive a Pentagon endorsement. It was almost 1985, over three years after I had left my previous church, that we gained full recognition and began placing men and women in the service. It was then that I began to realize the full extent of what the Lord had in mind for me and this mission.

We grew from having no chaplains in 1984 to having more than one hundred when the Gulf Crisis began, and almost half of these were in the reserves. These chaplains, both men and women, felt that they had been called to witness to and serve America, and they thought that their careers would be spent in peacetime service. None of them expected to see more than a half million men and women stationed in the Middle East preparing for a war that most predicted would be bloody and long. They had simply expected to be peacetime chaplains.

These men and women, like those chaplains of other denominations, felt called to serve both God and country, and they had not entered this service lightly or unprepared. They had been armed with four years of college plus three years of seminary. They had been ordained by Full Gospel Churches, and they had been active in Spirit-filled schools and congregations. They had proved their love for the Lord, and His presence in their hearts was obvious through their actions. They wanted and needed to help others find the joy and happiness that they had found, and they felt that God had a purpose for them in the military.

As the Full Gospel Chaplaincy program grew, I was proud of the way our men and women carried themselves and their message. They were Christian soldiers with a mission. They wanted to win the battle for truth, and they wanted to bring a new spirit to their flock.

As I traveled across the nation, appearing on national talk shows and in hundreds of churches, I spoke proudly of what the Lord had done in fulfilling His promise to me. I also was able to share with people the amazing changes our chaplains were witnessing throughout the military ranks. Men and women who had never known a moving, spirit-filled experience were being led to a new depth of understanding of God and His message. And this, I promised, was just the beginning. I sensed that the greatest impact of our work would come in the future.

Then I received the word, the same word that almost every citizen of the United States and the free world received—"We are going to the Gulf and we are going to drive Saddam out of Kuwait." Like many people across the country and around the world, I wondered what it meant and the effects the Persian Gulf conflict would have on the men and women serving there.

Almost all of my peers felt that economic sanctions and even eventual war would only serve to harden the resolve of Saddam and his battle-trained soldiers. Again and again I heard that the Arabs were fanatics who cared little about life and looked forward to a confrontation with us. I was also informed that we didn't understand an enemy like this one and that we would soon find ourselves in another Vietnam. This war, it was predicted, would again divide America and Americans.

Yet, deep down inside, I wasn't so sure. Something was different. I had been in constant contact with my men and women in the field who had been working side by side with all levels of the military. They had a confidence that I hadn't seen since World War II. The United States seemed to be interested not only in confronting an enemy, but in providing moral leadership. It was the latter that had been lacking for some time. For far too long, we had been content with telling people what they should do and how they should live, but we hadn't been providing examples. We now seemed ready to back up our words with actions.

In the early days of the conflict, I was hearing interesting reports from our chaplains. They acknowledged that much work had to be done and many people needed to be saved. Our troops felt strong, ready, and able to meet this challenge. They firmly believed that they were serving in the best military in the world and that they were quite prepared to do their jobs and do them well. While the question of preparedness was being raised again and again in the media, the common soldier's answer—the one that wasn't being presented by the press—was a resounding "Yes! We are ready!"

As good as I felt about our men and women, and as confident as I was about their abilities, I was also concerned that the confrontation with Saddam would be a bloody affair. I had seen firsthand men's reaction to death in combat, and I knew that most of our men and women hadn't. No matter how prepared they were as soldiers, this sight would cut at their insides and change them forever.

As more and more troops shipped out, and more and reservists were called up, I couldn't help but think back over my years of active service. I once again saw the faces of boys who had died before they had had a chance to taste the real sweetness of life. I remembered holding the hands of injured G.I.'s, knowing that I would be the last person to hear their voice and share their thoughts. I thought of the horrors of war, the times that were too terrible to even be a nightmare—the imagination could never dream up such pain and anguish. I remembered scenes I hadn't thought of in years. The final prayers of dying men—their very words—came back to me again and again.

Then I thought of the day in Germany. God had spoken because He had wanted to give me the chance to get ready for a time of revival. Over fifteen years before, He had set in motion an idea which would begin to be realized in the Persian Gulf. It took this long period of time for His words to be understood and for the humble human beings He was leading to implement His plan. God had been working all along so that, when the time was right, this ministry of His would be in place.

As August became September and more Americans were called to serve their country, I watched and listened. Our chaplains were requesting more Bibles and literature. The military men and women wanted more services than ever before. Many of them wanted to study in order to gain a greater understanding of God and His plan. We were getting reports of hundreds of soldiers being saved, countless others rededicating their lives, and thousands showing a genuine interest in finding out more about Jesus.

On the home front, members of Full Gospel Churches joined with people of all faiths in praying for our men and women overseas. Congregations were setting aside special services and initiating prayer circles. Men and women serving in the Persian Gulf who had never really talked with Christians were now receiving letters and postcards from committed men and women. Evangelism was being reborn in congregations that had not been spiritually active in years.

Even in our schools, children were writing to servicemen and women. Our children were praying for the soldiers and telling them that they were proud of them. They wanted the men and women serving overseas to be safe and to know that they were loved.

The American flag, along with the Christian cross, were common sights in windows, on clothes, and in cars. People were proud to say that they were praying for the people of our armed forces. Prayer was even being spoken of openly in the press and at business meetings.

It had taken a long time, but Vietnam's old wounds were being healed. In this nation's search for a new identity, we had rediscovered an old one—we are a country that trusts in God and believes that we are movers and shakers in His army. While to many observers the discovery of this new source of pride and purpose seemed like an overnight occurrence, I realized that it had been waiting to be discovered for a long time. We had just needed something or someone to awaken it. We had a thirst for the Gospel and for sharing it, but we hadn't gone to the well to drink.

When Saddam pushed us, we didn't pause to question ourselves. Instead we acted. We did the right thing—we stood up to the Baghdad Bully. Then as we prepared to confront him on our own terms, we fell to our knees to meet the Lord and learn about His terms.

Our military was prepared, and Saddam gave them a chance to prove their readiness. Thank God, our spiritual leaders were ready too. The next few months in the desert would see a revival the likes of which hadn't been seen in years. Our men and women in uniform would drink from the well of salvation, and no one would ever again have to ask about their spiritual preparedness. They were ready!

CHAPTER THREE

On the Home Front

"The U.S. troops recently sent to the Middle East have entered a world they're not completely prepared for. Even people familiar with the deserts of the American Southwest are surprised by the ferocity of the Saudi climate."

The Insider Report—Fall 1990

IN ATTEMPTING TO INFORM TROOPS AND THEIR DEpendents about what to expect upon deployment, military information departments issued long and detailed newsletters. Some of the information was useful, some was not; some items were interesting, others routine. Consider the following excerpt from the Fall 1990 *Insider Report*:

> The people of the Arab world, despite long centuries straddling major trade routes, have great difficulty accepting the ways of strangers, especially when the strangers are guests in their country.
> Military people heading for the Middle East will get lengthy briefings on the climate and the people of the Middle East. Here are a few things to mull over for military folks who expect to be sent there and for the family members left behind:

- Chapstick, skin ointment, and eyedrops are necessities.
- The Saudi desert is rough on wood and rubber. Thinking about taking a customized pen made from oak? Your favorite sunglasses for rugged times in the field have rubber frames? Come up with something else.
- Sunglasses also fall into the must-have category. If you wear prescription glasses, look into having more than one pair. Keep them in cases that will take some abuse.
- Alcohol and pornography aren't tolerated by strict Moslems, and Saudi Arabia is run by the strictest of the lot.
- The mixture of high humidity and ultra-fine sand plays havoc with electrical equipment and fine instruments. A couple of cheap transistor radios might be wiser than an expensive short-wave receiver.
- If you bring a camera, make it a cheap one and be very careful. Ask permission before taking a Saudi's picture. Don't photograph mosques, government buildings, or people praying. (page 1)

And the information, much of it needed and useful, went on and on. The report listed books for service personnel and their families to read so they could better understand the people and the religion of the area. Numerous books on Islamic religion were highlighted as well as some dealing with Jewish faith and culture, but the Bible did not make the recommended reading list. Ironically, it would be the book most requested, most turned to, and most read by members of the U.S. Armed Forces seeking useful information about how to cope with what they were facing. In fact, I think the Scriptures should have been classified under the heading "Basic Survival Skills and Equipment."

Another heading read "Family Routines Hurt by Deployment." A long list of things to do in order to help all family members through the tough times of separation followed. Therapy, planned outings, dialogue, and discussion were suggested, but there was no mention of prayer, church worship, or Bible reading. Religion was only mentioned in regard to the other guys!

With its silence on the subject of Christian faith, the literature being distributed seemed to ask the question "Was God really any more important now than He was a few months or weeks before?" A faithful, Spirit-filled Christian soldier would probably and rightly answer, "No. I need the Lord every moment of every day." But people who had never depended on His day-to-day guidance or had limited their view of His relevance to matters strictly concerning the church might find themselves turning to Him now more than ever before. These military personnel might find a reason to reach out to God, and they might hope and pray that someone would suggest the Bible as a valuable guide for tough times. That is why chaplains are in place and ready to supplement the outstanding military training of our men and women with some substantial spiritual training.

As the men and women of our armed forces headed for the Persian Gulf—in many cases leaving

behind empty churches as well as lonely families—
who would reach out to those left at home? Where
would they find the comfort they needed? And how
would the wives handle this tour of duty? It had
been a long time since the United States had been
forced to split up so many families in preparation for
war. Would they survive the separation? Were they
equipped to deal with the loneliness and the worry?

I once found an interesting description of military wives, and I've kept it in my files. It probably
says more than all of the armed forces literature in
existence. When I have been called away from my
home and family, I have turned to it. The passage always reminds me just how much a military wife
goes through when her spouse is away. It also points
out just how important these brave women are to
the people they love.

When God Created Military Wives

When the good Lord was creating military
wives, He was in His sixth day of overtime. An angel appeared and said, "You're having a lot of trouble with these. How are these different from the
standard model for wives?"

The Lord replied, "Have you seen the specifica-
tions? Each of these wives must be completely independent, but must be sponsored to get on post;
have the qualities of both mother and father during deployments; be a perfect hostess for four to
forty guests; handle emergencies without military
orders; cope with the flu and with transfers all

over the Earth; be able to convert 1400 hours to 2:00 p.m.; have a kiss that cures anything from a child's torn valentine to a serviceman's arduous duty; have the patience of a saint when waiting for a unit to return stateside; and have six pairs of hands."

The angel said, "Six pairs of hands? No way!"

The Lord answered, "Don't worry. Each will have other military wives to help. Besides, it is not only the hands that must be so special; it is also the heart. The heart of each military wife must swell with pride for the Armed Forces of the United States of America, sustain the ache of separations, bear on soundly when too tired to do so, and be able to say, 'I understand' when it doesn't and to say 'I love you' regardless."

"Lord," said the angel touching His sleeve gently, "go to bed. Rest. You can finish these military wives tomorrow."

"I can't," said the Lord. "I'm so close to creating something unique. Already I have military wives who can heal themselves when sick, feed unexpected guests who are stuck in the area due to bad weather, wave good-bye to husbands from a runway or a pier, and understand that it's important to the United States when a military husband must leave."

The angel then touched the military wives and sighed, "They are too soft."

"But tough," cried the Lord. "You cannot imagine what these wives can do or endure."

The angel ran a finger across the cheeks of all the wives and said, "There are leaks. I told you that you were putting too much into this type of wife."

"Those are not leaks," answered the Lord. "Those are tears."

"What are the tears for?" asked the angel.

"For joy, sadness, pain, loneliness, and pride. But," the Lord added somberly, "I did not put the tears there."

That story, probably written by a lonely military wife, expresses the feelings of hundreds of thousands of women when their men were shipped overseas. Many were deeply troubled, burdened by their worries and heartfelt pain, and in most cases, those hurting the most were women who did not know the Lord. Without faith, there is little hope, and without hope, there is no security. But the God who had a hand in creating military wives could also have a hand in helping them when their loved ones were overseas—if those wives knew Him.

In this war, men as well as women were left behind as spouses went to the front. In many cases, the departure of a wife and mother disrupted the home even more. Suddenly a man had to be a cook, a maid, a chauffeur, a nurse; he was forced to take on all the roles and perform all the tasks which he usually left to his mate. Military deployment in 1990 brought with it unique struggle and pain as men were left alone on the home front. How would these temporarily single-parent families react in the hour-to-hour, day-to-day waiting and hoping? Their reactions would reveal much about our country's spiritual preparedness.

How would these military dependents, left behind in the United States, be able to endure the days, weeks, and months of not knowing whether their families would ever be together again? In most cases, the words of the wives tell the story of a foundation of faith that had been in place long before the conflict and had in fact been strengthened by it.

Jane Ahl, the wife of a military chaplain, became terribly concerned as soon as talk of war began. She had questions, and she sought answers. Like most of us, she wondered how anything good could come from war and, on a more personal level, from separation from her husband. Her words, as well as her husband's response, seem typical of the strength and the faith of the families left at home.

I remember asking Ed in August what would happen if he had to go to war.

He said, "I will be so busy making sure that all of my troops are ready to go and have been taken care of, that I won't have time for much else."

I was somewhat taken aback because I had been asking about me and the children. When he figured out what was wrong, he apologized and said, "I know that God will take care of you because of your relationship with Him. You are mature enough to handle things. It's my soldiers that I'm not so sure about!'

Jane's husband was one of the Full Gospel chaplains who was called up early. He was eager to serve his country, and he wanted to make sure that his men were spiritually prepared for service. Still, it was tough for his wife and three children to watch him go even though they knew that he was doing what he had been called to do. It was only natural for them to wonder whether they would see him come home. Yet, because Jesus is Lord of their lives, they had a perspective and a strength that many others lacked.

We went to see Ed leave. The whole time my family was in an uproar with emotion, but Ed and I were at total peace. This was the change that God had told us about. I really believed that, if I had not been obedient to prayer when God told me to, I wouldn't have been able to handle this as well as I have. You see, God drew me closer to Him because He knew that I was going to need strength, help, support, and peace through this time.

We have found that what happened to Jane was hardly unusual. Just months before Saddam Hussein invaded Kuwait, she had begun to become more involved in prayer. She had felt called, even though she didn't understand why, to devote more of her life to communicating with God. And her obedience to that call paid off. When she needed to feel His hand on her, strengthening her and guiding her, He was there. She recognized the presence of the Lord, and she knew how to talk with Him. While many others were searching for answers, she knew where to go to find them.

This experience has allowed all of us to draw closer to God and have quality time with Him. The children and I have become closer, too. I have been able to walk in love more and more every day with them. I believe that God is using this time for us to get to know each other and to work on our relationships. God has been my husband, and He has been a father to the kids. When I have a problem, I go to God. He has the answers for me in everything I come up against.

Jane's letter was just one of hundreds that I received telling me of the same thing—God moving in people's lives. As I mentioned earlier, even before any military action had been initiated, churches, schools, community groups, and individuals were reaching out in support of our men and women in the Gulf. Signs saying, "We support our troops" were appearing in the windows of businesses and homes. Yellow ribbons and American flags seemed to be everywhere. Monday through Saturday, the streets were alive with people singing the praises of our brave servicemen and women.

Even more remarkable events were happening on Sundays. Churches of all denominations were welcoming record crowds. Men and women who hadn't been in God's house in years were coming back to listen to preachers, sing hymns, and pray. The flag-waving didn't die down after the first few weeks, and neither did the renewed enthusiasm for worship.

Most Americans could not remember a time when getting close to God seemed so important. The last time we had seen anything like this was during World War II. But why should we be surprised that it was happening again? After all, each of us feared we might lose a member of our family, a neighbor down the street, or a kid from church we'd watched grow up. With over a half million of our men and women sent to the Persian Gulf, and what many predicted would be the bloodiest war in modern history, we were all aware of how valuable and how fragile life is. We all felt a need to go back to our Lord and ask Him to protect these very precious gifts— the lives of our soldiers. We prayed persistently for God's help, guidance, and protection. Those left at home had their own battle—on the level of spiritual warfare—to fight in support of the soldiers.

Laurie Wayman, a pastor's wife, felt a double loss when her husband was called up. When he went to the Gulf, the pulpit was left open too. She not only had to be mother and father, but she also had to take over many duties at their church. Her story, like Jane's, was repeated many times across the country during the last few months of 1990.

Just before my husband was called up, [our church] had a Teen Mania crusade on a Tuesday night. Five souls were saved. It was a wonderful time. Then, on Wednesday morning, the call came for John to report in twenty-four hours. Needless to say, we were devastated.

Laurie and John's reaction was the same as tens of thousands of other people. But while the thoughts of separation hurt and they dreaded splitting their family (their three children range in age from just a few weeks to four years), they also realized that God could use John in the service. The Waymans knew that he was needed and that he would be able share the Good News of God's love with those who would be all too aware of the bad news of the world. With God at the center of their lives, John and Laurie were able to gain much from their time apart.

I have learned to appreciate my husband so much more, not only for what he does as my husband and our children's father, but also for what he does as a pastor since I am endeavoring to fill that role now too.

I have grown much closer to the Lord because I have had to. Reading my Bible and praying, worshiping God, and spending time in fellowship with Him have become a matter of survival. I know I cannot make it without Him.

The fact that my husband is able to minister there is a tremendous encouragement to me and our church folks. This gives them vision for the lost right here at home.

Even with her great spiritual strength, Laurie was further uplifted by the reactions of men and women she didn't know. Common Americans who supported our troops encouraged Laurie—and who knows how many more—time after time after time.

Sometimes I feel really alone. I really appreciate seeing people wearing or displaying yellow ribbons.

Dixey Behnken, one of our own chaplains, was also buoyed by the spirit of the American people. On his plane flight over, he was pondering how America had by and large forgotten how to witness, to evangelize, to reach out, to care, and even to pray. He was thinking about all those people who call themselves Christians but don't seem to take their faith very seriously. Then a woman on the plane touched his arm, asked him if he was a chaplain, and offered him her ideas about what was happening in the States because of the conflict in the Gulf.

On the jet I was talking to a lady of another faith and she said, "In our church, we have started having prayer every morning at 7:00 for soldiers in Saudi." I thought, "Wonderful, wonderful. God is stirring up His people."

This type of revival boosted the morale of chaplains from every denomination and motivated them to work even harder in the field. They knew that millions of Americans were actively praying for them, and this had never happened before on such a large scale. Beginning with wives, children, mothers, fathers, neighbors, and friends, this revival of prayer power had spread quickly into churches. From churches, it had moved to schools and even sporting events. Prayers were being said, and people were noticing.

I picked up a *Dallas Morning News* and saw on the front page a story of a husband and wife praying together on the phone just before he flew to Saudi. Editors in several major newspapers asked people to pray. It was becoming clearer and clearer to me that, in almost every facet of our lives, God was moving and, more miraculously, people were accepting Him.

Our troops in the Middle East had taken note of this, too. Many soldiers were so impressed by the millions who were praying for them, and by the tens of thousands who were sharing Scriptures in the letters they were writing, that chaplains were often approached with questions and requests as soon as they landed in Saudi. Men and women wanted to know more about salvation, the power of prayer, and the spiritual health of their own souls. These people knew that their mission in the Gulf had a purpose, but they wanted to make sure that their lives did, too. Life seemed out of control and the world on the brink of madness. Where else could they turn but to God?

It was becoming clear that the Persian Gulf

War was different from other recent wars. Families would indeed wait and support their soldiers, and while they waited, they would get involved in reaching out and touching lives. That is what revival is all about. That is what brings the power of the spirit to life. That is where Christian power begins.

Doris Bowers, a chaplain's wife, wrote a book for wives of chaplains. In it, she offers the following advice: "Be prepared to move frequently. Be positive about your husband's assignments. Ask God to be in charge and to put you where He wants you to be. Your neighborhood can be your personal mission field. If you consider each new move as an opportunity and adventure, your husband will praise you, and your children will catch your enthusiasm and be positive also."

This kind of positive attitude, first evident when Saddam invaded Kuwait and the world started to respond, began to open doors. The people who stayed behind were so inspired by the courage and determination, the faith and the strength of those they sent to battle that they took up their own battle gear and started sharing the story of Jesus in a very special way—people on the home front lived their faith. They took the Gospel message of hope to their neighbors, to chapel, to the unit, to the homes of friends, to their churches, to their clubs, to their family, and to the supermarket.

With these person-to-person, one-on-one expressions of love and concern, a huge spirit of revival began to move across the nation. Caught up in its power, men and women everywhere were saying, "God Bless America" and, for the first time in years, they were meaning it!

CHAPTER FOUR

A Thirst in the Desert

"I have received some cards with Psalm 91 printed on them. I've got my cards, I've got my crosses, I've got my Bibles . . . . I feel like I'm loaded for the Bear!"

Chaplain in Saudi—November 1990

IN A LARGE SUPERMARKET IN HILLSBORO, TEXAS, A hand-lettered poster, held up by a push pen and surrounded by announcements of garage sales and pets for sale, listed the needs of the men and women serving in the Persian Gulf. The poster asked shoppers to remember those in the armed forces by sending them things they needed, and an address was given. This simple sign drew a huge response. Item after item was purchased, carefully wrapped, and mailed halfway around the world from the local post office.

Generosity like this was not isolated or unusual. All across the United States, in the most populous cities and the most remote rural villages, the poorest and the wealthiest of America—men, women and children from every possible background—were responding to the needs of the troops. Packages by the truckload were shipped to New York and then forwarded to members of all branches of the service. The volume of items sent was huge! Were these gifts evidence of God moving in the hearts of the American people?

A fifth-grade girl in Alabama baked cookies, placed them in a tin, and then added a letter of encouragement to whoever received the package. A few weeks later, a serviceman far away from home was given the tin addressed simply to "A U.S. Army Soldier." Excitedly he opened it and discovered that his own daughter was the sender. The young girl's package had arrived safely in Saudi to be opened by—out of the half-million men and women stationed there—her own father, giving him the lift he needed. Was this merely a coincidence or was it the hand of the Lord?

In community centers, a welfare mother packed boxes alongside a banker's wife. They were different colors, they lived in vastly different parts of their community, and they traveled in different social circles. Neither had a son or daughter in the Gulf, but the two were linked by the feeling that they needed to help and by a sense of pride in their country and their servicemen and women. There, at a small table, these two strikingly different women found a common bond. Was this a miracle?

America's response to the war effort was like none since the 1940s. The letters from schoolchildren, the cookies, the toothpaste, the junk food, the tapes, and the paperback books had a tremendous impact on the troops overseas. But the items that disappeared the fastest were those which had some spiritual significance. The most basic human need was the greatest in the Gulf, and it was up to the American people to respond.

From the day our first chaplain arrived in the Persian Gulf, I began to receive cards and calls requesting items to help satisfy the soldiers' thirst for the Gospel message. Even before we could contact the churches and schools which help support us and tell them of our needs, they were calling us and asking what they could do. Was it just chance that so many people recognized a need before being asked to help?

With God's blessing, these churches and schools sent one hundred and fifty thousand crosses and then went to work getting the other needed items. The crosses were grabbed up as quickly as they were unwrapped by our chaplains. Men and women put them on chains, wore them around their necks with their dog tags, carried them in their pockets, and slept with them in their hands.

For G.I.'s and officers alike, these small crosses that represented their Christian faith—bought with a donation of just ten cents—became all the more important because they were fighting in a land where Christianity is not welcome. Our American soldiers were not free to express their faith or to worship as they did in America. Without this freedom they came to appreciate the real gift of choice.

After shipping the first batch of crosses, individuals of all ages continued to wonder what they could do. We responded by saying, "Keep up the giving—and write letters to let the soldiers know that they are loved and that you are praying for them." We didn't have to ask twice.

Students in Christian schools set up class competitions to see who could bring in the most dimes for crosses. When they shipped the crosses overseas, the children wrote letters to the chaplains who were to receive them. In these notes, they expressed hope, love, and respect in ways that only young children can. When chaplains shared these notes, the words touched the hearts of big, tough soldiers who might have thought themselves immune to the ramblings of a child.

One student wanted the troops to become like super Ninja Turtles with flak jackets, helmets, and a Bible. When the soldiers first heard this, most of them smiled and a number laughed out loud, but many picked up Bibles on their way out. Other children suggested that, when they were asleep, the soldiers hold their crosses like shields. Those facing combat understood just what kind of shield the message behind the Cross could be.

In January, Colonel David P. Peterson, the United States Central Command Chaplain at Operation Desert Shield headquarters, wrote me expressing his thanks for our gift of crosses. In his letter, he said, "As you remember from your Vietnam days, crosses are extremely important to our Christian servicemembers. Your devotion will be greatly appreciated and will surely enhance the ministry of our chaplains. Thank you for your loyal support and concern. God bless you as you continue to labor for our Lord."

I was extremely proud of that tribute, but I wished each man, woman, and child who had sacrificed something in order to share these crosses with the men and women in the Persian Gulf could have received the same letter. Better yet, I wish they could have seen the powerful effect that their gifts were having on our people in the region.

As important as the crosses were, it was the gift of the Bibles that seemed to be most needed and most eagerly accepted. Hardly a worship service was held where scores of men and women didn't request a new Bible. It was easily the most widely read book in the desert. Right in the middle of the kingdom of Islam, the Good Book was Number One! Even veteran chaplains were overwhelmed by the enthusiasm of their flocks. These people actually wanted to study their Bibles. This practice, often ignored in both the military and at home, was becoming a routine for military personnel on both land and sea. The Bible, God's written Word for men and women to read, was having a profound and very personal impact on those reading it as the world readied for war.

As one chaplain's Bible study concluded and scores of men left a crowded tent to hike across the sand, two rough-looking soldiers approached him. At first they held back while he spoke to other men, and they watched as he handed out some tracts and tapes. As they stood waiting, they listened to two Christian men share news from their wives back in the States, and then they waited as the chaplain looked at some photos that a private had brought of his kids.

The two men, perhaps in their mid-twenties, almost left the tent, but something was working on them. They stayed and continued to wait their turn—and they had to wait quite a while. A host of folks wanted to ask questions and share news with the chaplain.

The fact that these particular men had come to the study was something of a miracle. To them, religion had always seemed like a crutch for the weak, something for the cowardly. Tough and street-wise, they had gotten by on meanness as they grew up, and they had the scars to prove that they could handle just about anything from anyone. They had always claimed to be afraid of nothing, the toughest of the tough, but now they wondered if they had the guts to ask one simple question. They may never have worked up the courage, but the chaplain had noticed them standing to his right, somewhat hidden in a dark corner.

As the chaplain finished taking a prayer request, he walked in their direction. "Do you men want something?"

For almost thirty seconds, they fidgeted and looked at each other rather sheepishly. Finally one of them mumbled, "Can you give us a big Bible Chaplain?"

"What?" the chaplain replied, unable to understand the softly spoken words.

"You know," the other chimed in. "A big Bible. All they gave us in basic training was a little one.

But we're supposed to go into combat soon, and we want a big Bible."

The chaplain, a man I know very well, pulled a couple of Bibles out of a box. He approached the two men, smiled, and reached out to shake their hands.

"I guess what you mean is one with both the New and Old Testaments. Is that right?"

They nodded their heads.

"Well," the chaplain continued, "we have some Bibles here that some folks back in the States just sent me. I have both the King James and the Revised Standard Version. The King James is called the Authorized Version by some people, and the Revised is often referred to as the R.S.V."

The two soldiers turned to each other and whispered back and forth. Then one said, "We want the R.S.V.P. version."

Funny? Yes and no. These were spiritually illiterate young Americans doing the best they knew to start a search for God. And isn't there a sermon here? Hasn't God indeed extended to us "an invitation" to which we should RSVP?

The chaplain—and others like him—met hundreds of soldiers like these two. Many of them now sleep with their new Bibles clutched in their hands. It was as if they had been searching all their lives for what this Book contains, and now, in the middle of a scorpion-filled desert as the world prepared for war, they had found it. This episode in international politics which affected them so personally had enabled them to see the light and humbled them enough to accept the help that was always there.

The two soldiers walked towards the door of the tent, still tightly holding their Bibles with both hands and wearing a new expression of calm on their faces. Right before they left, they turned and waved. The most expressive of the two said, "Tell whoever sent these, 'God bless 'em.'"

The chaplain nodded.

This true story is typical of thousands which tell of a soldier's desire for his or her own copy of God's Word. Bibles sent by Christians in the United States to our service personnel in the Gulf were the hottest items around, the most asked for, and the most joyfully received. And, interestingly, in one of the dustiest places on the planet, these Bibles—unlike most that are in homes throughout the U.S.—were gathering no dust. They were being read and studied. For the moment, the Moslem nation of Saudi Arabia was the greatest Christian mission field on earth.

Also gladly received by our soldiers overseas were Christian tapes—music as well as humor, study, and sermon tapes. The servicemen and women were devouring anything that had to do with the Christian faith. They wanted to learn more about God and understand more about Jesus. They simply weren't satisfied with a little knowledge—they felt like they needed it all and needed it now!

Why was this happening? Was it simply the fear of death, the closeness of actual battle, that prompted their interest in God and His Word? This had to be one factor, but in Korea and Vietnam, escaping through the use of drugs or alcohol was a more common way of dealing with fear than trying to discover the meaning of life and faith in the Bible. So more than just fear had to be motivating this interest in things spiritual.

From what they've told me, I know that our chaplains were deeply moved by the Spirit and the faithful support of the American people. For the first time in years, we seemed to truly be a *United* States, and we were united under God. The letters and packages sent to troops clearly reflected this. Those letters and packages also showed our young servicemen and women that we cared for them. So beyond fear, I think it was the genuine and active concern of their fellow American Christians and the call to prayer from our country's leaders that prompted servicemen and women by the thousands to seek God.

The fact that hundreds of thousands of churches were holding special prayer services, writing letters, and donating Bibles, books, tapes, and crosses introduced a new kind of thinking to the men and women on the front. They began to sense some kind of spiritual link to a family. These military personnel—all volunteers—were being prayed for individually and collectively. They knew that they were being lifted up, and if they didn't already understand why or what that meant, these prayers caused them to wonder. When they wondered, they began to ask questions, and the person who asks questions usually finds answers.

Unknowingly, and surely unwittingly, Saddam Hussein had sparked a spiritual revival in churches and Christian homes all across the nation. If our men and women were going to fight the man considered today's Hitler, then we wanted our troops to know that we were behind them and supporting them with our prayers. It is a fact that true revival begins when prayer is joined with action, and never before had I seen such united prayer and such concerted action on such a wide scale.

In helping Kuwait and our allies in the Middle East defeat an evil and power-hungry dictator, we opened a new pipeline. This one was not filled with oil. Instead, this pipeline was filled with love—God's love. Half a world away from their homes, men and women from the United States were experiencing a rebirth of the Christian spirit. This rebirth may not have happened without Saddam, and it definitely couldn't have happened without those on the home front providing the Bibles and the prayers which would enable our troops to find God.

CHAPTER FIVE

Women on the Front Lines

THE PERSIAN GULF WAR MARKED A SIGNIFICANT first in American military history: for the first time ever, women were assigned to potential battlefront positions. The United States asked females in uniform to lay down their lives for their country. While this type of service is not completely unknown in some nations, women had not been considered a part of the American fighting force in any earlier war.

In the past, our military women have served as nurses and secretaries. While they were sometimes assigned duties as drivers or pilots, they were always assigned to noncombat situations. In 1990, however, as an all-volunteer force was deployed to Saudi, women were shipped in as active members of all facets of the military operation. Things had definitely changed.

The chaplaincy is another area of military service long thought of as "for men only," yet many of the Lord's finest servants in this war were actually women. While the news media did not offer much coverage about this historic situation, women chaplains did indeed play an important role in supporting our soldiers on the front lines. Letters from these outstanding women crossed my desk daily, and the effects that they had on the soldiers in Saudi were profound. The effect their ministry had on me as I saw God use them was also profound.

I was raised in a denomination which didn't allow women in the pulpit, and for many years I served in that denomination. During those years, however, my partner in life—my wife—had a vital ministry of her own as she shared the Gospel with men and women all over the world. She was called by God, led by the Spirit, and worked hard to expand her Savior's kingdom on a daily basis. Nowhere was there anyone who prayed more sincerely, witnessed more openly, or was more obviously meant to do the Lord's work than Charlene Ammerman. She inspired me to begin to think of the many ways that women can do God's work and fit into His plan in both the military and nonmilitary world. Her example helped open my eyes, and I found a new vision for women in ministry.

To a large degree, we *men* of God have been behind the times in recognizing just what the *women* of God can do, even though the evidence has always been right under our noses. A look at the Gospels and Acts reveals the status which Jesus granted women and the important role of women in the work of the church. Jesus ministered to women when other people would not approach them. He assured them that they had a place in God's plan and that their lives counted for something very special. He knew that a woman can lead in ways a man cannot, and He recognized that a woman can communicate and encourage in ways that a man cannot. Women ministered to Jesus Himself, and they were active in the growth of the early church. Yet many people did—and still do—ignore the example Christ set for us by his interaction with women.

But I couldn't ignore it for long. My wife had so many gifts that could have come from no other source than the Holy Spirit. She was especially blessed in discernment and counsel. So many times I have watched her spend time with a brokenhearted serviceman and be used by God to restore his faith. She has helped put together lives that most of us had written off as forever broken. She has the ability to find hope in despair and potential in the most limiting circumstances. She has a way of calming and comforting, of turning a person's eyes inward, and then allowing the Lord to work in a quiet, powerful manner. She does all these things in ways that I cannot.

As I have watched her on television and listened to her on radio, I realize that, being a woman, she reaches men and women in a much different manner than men do. Maybe it is because she is able to offer a degree of mothering along with her strong Christian witness. A mother's sensitivity and compassion are so important in the healing and learning process, yet how often we have ignored this need in both the military and nonmilitary ministry, in times of war as well as in times of peace.

I became so deeply moved by Charlene's heart for God and His people that I asked her to speak in pulpits as I traveled around the world. She won many converts in New Zealand, Australia, Hawaii, Korea, Europe, and the Philippines. When we came home to the United States, her speaking had equally moving results. Christ's kingdom was being enriched and enlarged through this woman's work. I knew that we needed more like her.

When she wasn't working directly with me in churches, she was serving as the Protocol Officer for the U.S. Army's largest Officer's Wives Club. Her Christian witness there was as strong as it would be in any church. As she led many women to read the Bible, pray, and witness, she was opening the door for Christ to be in military homes on an everyday basis.

When I founded the Chaplaincy of Full Gospel Churches, I knew who had to be by my side. Charlene thus became the Associate Director, and she has contributed greatly to what the organization has been able to accomplish.

While other denominations had problems finding men to do the Lord's work in the military, the Full Gospel Chaplaincy has been reviewing hundreds of requests to serve from both men and women. No doubt a large reason for these enthusiastic inquiries is the life and example of Rev. Charlene Ammerman, D.D.

At the same time that Charlene shows women that we have a place for them in our service, she is showing them that God has a place for them as well. So, at a time when the military was actively opening its doors to females and encouraging them to become one of America's best, we were there doing the same in the chaplaincy. We were proving that there was a place in this man's spiritual army for a woman who felt called by God.

And opening the chaplaincy to women came none too soon. The Gulf War placed an extreme amount of pressure on both men and women, and helping people deal with this pressure—a kind of pressure not felt in over a generation—would prove a tremendous challenge for our spiritual leaders. Among the people feeling the strain of the battlefield were people—both men and women—who couldn't or wouldn't respond to a strictly male voice. In many cases, without our women, these lost souls might never have been reached.

One eighteen-year-old G.I. met one of our female chaplains during a devotional. Frantic, the soldier had tears in her eyes and a deep fear in her heart. She didn't know what to do, what to think, or where to turn.

"I just joined so that I could get money for college," she explained to our sympathetic chaplain. The soldier's dark brown eyes welled to overflowing as she continued. "I mean, I never thought we would go to war or anything. None of us took the military service as being that serious. Now some of us may die. This is the real thing, and I never thought I would have to face it."

Looking at our caring chaplain, she then begged, "Will you please pray with me?"

By the time the evening was over, this young woman had been reintroduced to the faith she had known as a child. She admitted that it took a woman to touch her heart, to remind her—as her mother always had—that God is with us everywhere. Without our young chaplain, who knows the fear and the pain that this woman would have experienced? Now she is sharing her strength with others.

Scenes like this were repeated over and over again as men and women readied for action. We saw time and time again how a woman's touch can bring hardened souls back to the fold. For many old-time military men as well as long-time preachers, this was a bit shocking, but I had been seeing it come for a long time.

Time and time again, for instance, Chaplain Beverly Parry's ministry had inspired me and touched my heart. She is one of our most gifted servants and has a remarkable ability to bring the full measure of Christian faith to people's lives.

One young man in the Gulf, just an average soldier, was witnessing up a storm. Whenever he met someone, he would talk about what God had done for him. He had once been an alcoholic, a career soldier who was going to end his service as a drunk with a pension. Then Beverly began witnessing to him. She led him to the Holy Spirit and baptized him. That was two and half years before the events which led to the Gulf War, but the full fruit of saving that one soul came in the hot deserts in early 1991. This man personally led several soldiers to Jesus and helped countless others who had severe alcohol dependency problems.

Beverly has drawn others out of occult practices, drug habits, and demonic worship. Beverly can move sensitively and effectively in a world where men have so often failed. She listens to people, she comforts them as only a woman can, and she witnesses with the boldness of a preacher. With the Lord's strength and a mother's insight and love, she is touching souls in ways that no man could.

In one of her letters, she summed up the situation and the potential for revival as well as any of our chaplains. I shared her thoughts time and time again as I addressed our congregations.

It's an unprecedented situation over here. There's a lot of anxiety and anticipatory grief. A lot of lives that were unstable before are totally shaken now. But in the midst of this vacuum, this insecurity, there is a hunger. There is a real openness to the Gospel. People have a desire to know the truth, to have something to believe in, to have something to hold them up. You may have heard this from other chaplains, but what I see, spiritually, is that God needed American forces because in American forces there are Christians who can pray and break through the spirit of Islam and the anti-Christian mind-set of these nations.

This is an exciting time. When we speak of the Gospel, men and women hang on our every word. The men and women of the military are getting right with God. Maybe He allowed Saddam to be used for this purpose.

Beverly and women like her were going into an area where females were generally treated like second-class citizens, if not a lower form of life. In most Arab societies, women have no rights. In Saudi Arabia, they aren't even allowed to drive cars. So, not only was it unusual to see women acting in important military roles in this region, it was also completely unheard of to have them serve as spiritual leaders. We Americans were presenting role models the Saudis had never seen—and let me assure you that these new role models worked hard and impressed all those who watched them.

The work load women chaplains carried in the Gulf was equal to that of any man. They filled sandbags, dug trenches, helped unload trucks, and learned all the basics of protection—besides fulfilling their spiritual duties. And those spiritual responsibilities meant sharing hundreds of private devotions each week, preparing for as many as six different worship services daily, planning Bible studies, and offering individual counseling time. Sleep soon become a luxury and an option, and usually when they got it, it was only in short bursts. Men and women often roused the chaplains in the middle of the night to talk about spiritual issues. With over twenty-five percent of the military overseas making some type of spiritual decision for Christ, plus all the soldiers who were already believers, there was much work to be done by our chaplains.

The women in the chaplaincy, however, felt some pressure which the men didn't. Even though the world has changed a great deal, the women still had to prove themselves worthy of their positions. Many who were watching them expected them to crack under the battlefield pressure or fall short in some way. The women were often viewed under a microscope with those observing hoping they would fail. Our female chaplains were also challenged by the hardened soldiers who ordinarily had little time for any chaplain's words—but a woman really made them ill at ease. How could they take advice or counsel from a "girl"?

These "girls" worked hard, though, and they earned the respect of the soldiers they were ministering to. The results of their hard work—the thousands of souls who were saved and the many more who were comforted and encouraged—speak for themselves. The bottom line was that the women chaplains were needed on the battlefield, and we probably won't ever go to war again without them being there.

Beverly, a chaplain stationed right on the front lines, was one of the women who made an impact on people's lives that will be felt for years. Her drive, her determination, and her enthusiasm for her work was typical of what we heard from all of our female chaplains.

Sunday really sneaks up on me quickly here with all the work-space visitation and other duties of the week. I am doing about 50 devotions each week—can you imagine? All in all, this is the most exciting and fulfilling ministry I have ever done. And you know things are going well when people start helping your ministry happen without you even asking. The chapel tent just appeared, and so did the beginnings of a sound system.

I've recruited a choir, "The Saudi Voices of Praise." They are a down-home Gospel group—and they can really sing! It turns out that the petty officer has all kinds of talent.

I am also doing combat stress classes. Ministering to thousands of Marines and being heard by generals is something that would have been hard to imagine just a few weeks ago . . . . I feel I am in the palm of God's hand. It can't get much better than that! I shall have many exciting stories to tell my grandchildren.

The women in our military had an important role to play in the Gulf revival. Why? Because the soldiers in this war were both men and women, and these men and women were seeing God in a new light and often meeting Him for the first time. The women, though, were also seeing in our female chaplains flesh-and-blood reminders of how the Lord can use them to share the Gospel message.

Two thousand years ago, Christ had a vital place for women in His ministry. Far from taking them for granted, He encouraged women to use their gifts for

His glory, and the women around Him responded. But in today's world, women are, to a large degree, oppressed, and nowhere is this more true than in the Arab sphere of influence. But, as Americans were coming to rescue an innocent country from the hold of an evil dictator, people in the Arab nations were seeing women help—in both the physical and the spiritual sense—restore peace to the Islamic world.

When the Lord opened the door for women to take an active and significant role in spiritual warfare as well as military combat, He was enabling His forces to have a greater impact than ever before. The full participation of women was a very effective way to open the hearts of many Americans and the eyes of many Muslims. Consider the words of one of our female chaplains:

I never thought I'd be in a war—but I'm glad I'm here. If ever God has given me a task, this is it! My heart is blessed each day with the rewards of grace and laughter in people's lives. War is no fun, but I'm convinced that our country is doing the right thing and for the right reasons. God is richly blessing this work!

CHAPTER SIX

Doing Battle on Our Knees

God has no mercy on one who has no mercy for others.
An Arab Proverb

AS MORE AND MORE TROOPS LEFT FOR THE MIDDLE East, the American people stood strong in support of their military and behind the leadership of the United Nations, and the world focused its attention sharply on Saddam. His every move was studied, and his words were monitored. He was center stage in an international theater, and he was reveling in the spotlight.

At one point, we saw Saddam mingling with his "guests," the foreign nationals he held hostage as protection against attack. Such despicable actions made us more firmly resolved to no longer tolerate a despot's rule in any country, much less one that could threaten the world order and the international economy. Not since World War II, when countries around the globe united against Hitler's dictatorship and the Japanese tyranny, had so many different governments and cultures come together to fight a common enemy. Back then, we were the leader in the fight, but much of the world order had changed in the intervening years. One thing hadn't, though: the United States was still the force that the world looked to when peace was endangered.

In the recent past, the statement "I wonder what the U.S. will do about it" was spoken in a tone of taunting skepticism, if not distrust. The people of most nations wanted us to stay out of their affairs. The "Yankee go home" theme has been voiced countless times in the past two decades. Yet I wonder if we didn't bring this attitude—almost a type of ridicule—on ourselves. Had we been working from the wrong agenda when we dealt with other countries? Were we more interested in dollars and cents than morals and justice? I will leave those bigger questions to historians and philosophers, but I will take a stand on the Persian Gulf situation. In Kuwait, the choice was clear. We didn't have the kind of questions and doubts that plagued us in Vietnam. We knew that an injustice had been done, and we felt we should do something about it. And we had been invited to do so.

Many people in this country were excited about the opportunity to show off our military might. Many saw this moment as a chance to once again become the "heavyweight champion of the world." And while I could see that happening as a result of the events that were being played out, by October I was clearly seeing something even more important going on.

From the letters I received and the calls I got from our chaplains, a spiritual revival seemed to be underway—and it was a revival like none I had ever heard of. I was excited and even jubilant, but I waited as the weeks rolled by to see if this trend would continue or if the numbers would level out. Various people warned me that renewed interest in spiritual matters was merely a reaction to being away from home. They predicted that it would pass and that our G.I.'s would go back to being the hard-living, hard-fighting soldiers modeled after John Wayne. So I quietly waited and watched. As time went by, my instincts proved correct. The movement grew not only in the Middle East, but also here at home. God certainly seemed to be at work.

National as well as local media noted the unexpected upsurge in church attendance. It was reported that more than forty percent of the public was attending church in any given week, the greatest number since World War II. It seemed obvious that the country's climate was changing and, with it, the spiritual needs of the American people. After more than forty years of diminishing interest—a period of wandering in spiritual darkness—we were once again seeking truth. In the shadow of the "Me" generation, and in our present-day society of "Yuppies" who seem satisfied by material things, a growth of interest in the spiritual was being observed and documented. Was the war the only reason people were pursuing God?

World events over the past two years had certainly changed our thinking. The actions of governments and leaders halfway around the world were directly affecting us in ways that we hadn't felt since the 1930s. People we thought would never be granted the power of free speech were gaining it and, more importantly, were exercising it. What had begun as a church-backed labor movement in Poland, for instance, had ripped at the very heart of communism throughout Europe.

In other areas of concern, our government was leading the way in the stand against racism and injustice in South Africa. Americans were trying to help save orphans in Rumania and feed starving masses in Ethiopia. We once again cared about the international family of man, and we wouldn't mind if others noticed that we cared. Our world had been changing.

And, even if we weren't shouting it from the hilltops, many of us felt that God had to be moving for so much to be happening around the globe. As a result, we were attempting to follow His lead. Still, we needed a cause to really unite us and move us to act.

Saddam gave us that cause in August of 1990. Kuwait was a rich country, a nation which had used American technology and people to build a strong economic base. Even though Kuwait had fewer than two million people, its huge oil reserves made it a mighty player in the international business community. Although the United States had provided much assistance for its development, Kuwait was still a diamond in the rough. Because we hadn't taken our ideas of democracy and faith to the area (while welcoming our technology, Kuwait had strictly forbidden Christian theology to be introduced within its boundaries), the country hadn't grown with the kind of strength that could sustain it through the tough times. Then the unthinkable happened.

America has always hated bullies, and it was a bully who awakened our moral outrage and spurred our need to reach out to the victim. Just as we had seen in Hitler, we saw in Saddam the dangerous combination of ego, power, and anti-Christian leadership. We realized how important it was to live by the standard which Jesus set; we saw a real-life situation where living by the Golden Rule might have saved lives. As the Soviets had recently discovered, a government without spiritual guidance is one that must rule by tyranny. Such a place was Iraq.

As we grew closer to confrontation, I heard one of our chaplains speak. His words helped a great many of us begin to understand that all of the things which had happened and were happening were a part of God's plan and that this was a time of revival. Although he spoke to us at the beginning of the conflict, Dave Plummer's remarks and insight seem even more noteworthy now. I share some of his ideas here.

I believe that God is calling us to a holy war at this time in the Middle East. We hear Saddam Hussein announce that this is a holy war—and I believe him. But I don't believe that this is a holy war like any Saddam is aware of, and I don't believe that this is the blood-and-guts kind of war that most of us think about. Still, I do think that this is a holy war, and I want to see us do a little battling.

In Ephesians 6:10-13 we read, "Finally, be strong in the Lord and in his mighty power. Put on the full armor of God so that you can take your stand against the devil's schemes. For our struggle is not against flesh and blood, but against the rulers, against the authorities, against the powers of this dark world and against the spiritual forces of evil in the heavenly realms. Therefore put on the full armor of God, so that when the day of evil comes, you may be able to stand your ground." (NIV).

Who is the enemy? Some of us are thinking that the enemy is Saddam Hussein, the Iraqi people, or maybe the people in Iran, Jordan, even Turkey or Syria. In order to clarify the situation, allow me to relate a true story.

When World War I broke out, the war ministry in London dispatched a coded message to one of its outposts located in one of the most inaccessible areas of Africa. The message read, "War declared. Arrest all enemy aliens in your district."

The war ministry received this message in reply: "Have arrested ten Germans, six Belgians, four Frenchmen, two Italians as well as several Austrians and Americans. Please advise immediately as to whom we are at war with."

The British soldiers at this outpost had immediately gone out and arrested any foreigner they could grab. They weren't sure who they were at war with, but they wanted to make sure and get everything and everyone so that they would have the enemy covered.

So, more than seventy years later, who are we really at war with? This may sound very radical, but down deep, if you cut through the political issues of Iraq invading Kuwait and you get to the core of the war itself, I believe that our enemy is a spiritual one. I believe that "we wrestle not with flesh and blood."

While it might appear that we are wrestling with a living and mortal enemy, I think that what we are seeing in the war is a spiritual confrontation. This is a spiritual battle, one that God expects us to fight and win. It is an opportunity, and we cannot back down.

This spiritual battle has been raging for some time, and it just happened to spill out upon Saddam Hussein and the Iraqi people. Unfortunately for the Kuwaiti people, as well as their neighbors, they were in Saddam's vision and plans. And so it began.

While the military is doing its best to fight a battle, the source of the problem is not a physical or political issue; rather it is a spiritual one. You can send in all the wonderful A-10s, Stealth Bombers, Tomcats, F-16s, field artillery, defensive machines, amphibious assault forces—and none of them will be as effective as a Christian soldier on his or her knees doing spiritual battle. I mean that sincerely. The real power to change this region, to change each of our lives, to change the very country in which we live, is in prayer. Pray for peace, pray for protection for our troops. We need that sort of prayer. Through it lies victory!

There are principalities and authorities over this region of the world. There are fearsome demons who have come together there. Someone told me recently that they think that the demon warlord which had been over Germany for so long had been driven out when the "wall came tumbling down." I believe that Christians' prayers and praise helped bring that wall down, and I believe that Christians drove that demon out by the power of the Holy Spirit.

Do you know that people are saying that this same demonic spirit is now alive in Iraq? Considering the actions of Saddam, I can understand their thinking. Even the secular press is comparing him to Hitler. So, if the demon is there, can we do something about it? Yes! We can drive him out without a single drop of blood falling!

I believe that we can do something that even our troops cannot do. We can make prayerful intercession. As our prayers go up, His power comes down to command and control the demons and principalities that are challenging His will and our people. With God comes strength to conquer all evil, and this situation will allow us to present this fact to the world. Through prayer we will see a miracle—you can count on it!

Actually a miracle has already happened! Isn't it exciting to realize that, for the first time in over sixteen hundred years, Christians are being asked to come into a Muslim country? Think about that for a moment. Here is a place that has not heard the Gospel of Jesus Christ since the time Islam came into being, and we are right there.

Imagine for a moment the darkness that is there. Imagine the collection of demons and spiritual authorities that are gathered in that part of the world? It is an evil paradise, a place for the dark forces to rest, to inhabit, to control people for evil. And into that place, Christians have been invited.

When I read the Scriptures, it is clear to me that God loves all His people. I believe that God wants us to pray for the Muslim countries and, specifically, for the Christians who are preaching

Rebecca Purser watching her daddy, Chaplain Duane Purser, aboard the *USS Worden* as the ship sets sail out of Pearl Harbor, bound for Saudi Arabia.

Above: Chaplain Mark Johnston praying with marines during training exercises.

Left: Jim and Charlene Ammerman.

Just two days before the air war over Iraq began, these soldiers gathered to pray for their commander.

A Christmas tree decorating a tent chapel in Saudi Arabia.

Chaplain David Waters serving with the XVIII Airborne Corps Artillery.

Chaplain Jim Ammerman (Ret.), President and Director of the Chaplaincy of the Full Gospel Churches, presenting the Chaplaincy's flag to Chaplain Douglas T. Smith, Deputy Commander of the Army Chaplain's School. Photo by Russ Meseroll.

Above: Chaplain James Agnew conducting services in a warehouse.

Below: Marines embarking for training exercises at Camp LeJeune, North Carolina.

Chaplain Arley Longworth, U.S. Army, 24th Mechanized Division, with Major General John P. McDonough, USAF Chief of Chaplains in Saudi Arabia.

Chaplain David Waters taking his oath of office, officially beginning his ministry as a chaplain.

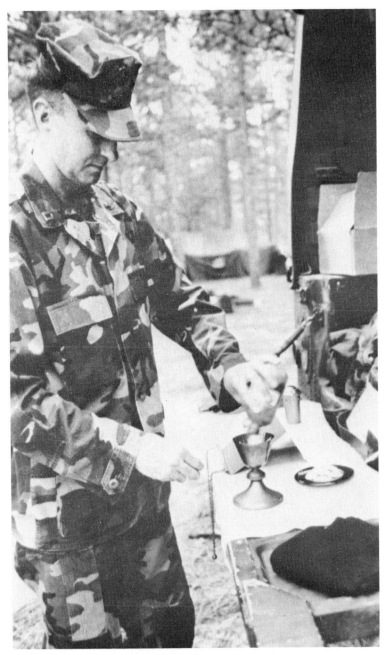

Chaplain Mark Johnston serving communion.

Chaplain David Waters baptizing a soldier in a decontamination tank in Saudi Arabia.

Chaplain Edwin Ahl praying with a soldier.

Chaplain Duane Purser.

Chaplain Klon K. Kitchen aboard the *USS Sylvania* in the Red Sea in support of Operation Desert Storm.

the Gospel to our troops. Did you know that hundreds are accepting Christ as Lord and Savior each day? A revival among the troops is breaking out. Americans are getting saved in the Gulf because they are fearful of what is ahead. Sometimes the Lord uses dangerous situations to get our attention. In addition, can you imagine the effect that these new Christians, supported by our prayers, can have on the people of the region? I believe God's Spirit would come down as He has never come down in history. We would see miracles like we have never seen.

Do you have any idea what the results of such movement and power would be? It would convert followers of Islam to Christianity. Followers of Islam do not believe in miracles. Even Mohammed never claimed to work a single supernatural act, so you can see what the miraculous power of salvation could do for Islamic people. Can you imagine what a born-again, spirit-filled Christian convert from Islam would be like? Can you imagine the power he would have? Can you imagine the effect? A revival could sweep through the entire region from this single conversion. Repeat this experience time and time again—and just think what could happen! We have a tremendous opportunity, one that history has never offered us before.

I believe that a revival of gigantic proportions can happen. And when it does, people will put down their guns and say, "Lord, save me. I'm yours." Then peace can come to the region. The best way to keep the Hitlers of the world out of power is to put Christ in the hearts of men and women.

We have so much to offer. In the religion of Islam a person is never a child of God; he is a slave to God. They don't feel the special privilege and closeness to the Lord that we Christians feel as we rest in the knowledge that we are God's children. Muslims don't feel love. We are taught to love our neighbors as ourselves, but they are taught to hate everyone except fellow Muslims—and then to not even trust them.

I believe that the Lord is calling His church to do spiritual warfare in the Middle East—but not just so American troops will triumph over Saddam Hussein. I think God is calling His church to spiritual warfare so that Arabs will fall to their knees in the knowledge that Jesus is their Lord. I want to see men dropping their weapons and falling on their knees in an effort to claim what is free for the asking—salvation through Jesus Christ. I don't want to hear about the slaughter of hundreds of thousands. I want to hear about the conversion of millions.

It can happen. It is beginning right now!

As Dave concluded his speech, it struck me that the real war was just beginning. We were to not only minister to half a million American service men and women, but also to begin a revival among the Islamic nations. Our influence had been asked for, even welcomed. We were there to act on the side of justice. We were once again respected and looked to as a beacon for justice, freedom, and hope. We were there not only to save these people from Saddam, but to offer them a better way of life and to share with them the hope of forgiveness and eternal life.

Excitement charged my soul as I thought about the possibilities of such a movement. Dave was right, the time was right, and now we would see just how far this revival would spread. I quickly bowed my head and asked the Lord, "In these days when You are doing so much, I pray that You will count me in and not count me out."

I then prayed that thousands—no, make that millions—of others would feel just as strongly about this special moment in time as Dave and I did. Saddam was no Islamic leader. He didn't even follow the religion's code of conduct. So maybe his people were ready for leadership that embraced a living, loving, and moral God, a God who loved them as much as He loved the men and women who were lined up in the sights of their Scud missiles.

CHAPTER SEVEN

Peering into the Face of Death

"I'm not scared of the Republican Guard or anything else that Saddam wants to throw at us. What I am scared of is dying. I don't want to die. There are too many things I haven't done."

An American Soldier—December 1990

AS THE UNITED NATIONS DEADLINE WAS SET AND Iraq was given a timetable for pulling out of Kuwait, the fearful reality of going to war began to hit those in the Gulf and at home. Like thousands of our American soldiers, we at home were afraid of what might happen and how many men and women would die, and we wondered if we would be able to face an enemy that had sworn to fight us to the death. We didn't have any answers—and we wouldn't have them unless there was actual combat. A cloud of worry seemed to hang over people, and they couldn't go anywhere to escape it.

In sports terminology, however, the ball remained in Saddam's court as the January 15 deadline neared. As the leaders of the allied forces considered their options and the possibility of defeating him, he enjoyed the spotlight. He was playing with us, taunting us, daring us—and then bragging that we did not have the stomach or faith to face him on his terms. He was making his stand in an attempt to become the ruler of the Arab world; he wanted to prove to all those who followed Islam that he could stand up to the whole world and win.

Even though military experts knew that Iraq couldn't possibly win in a war against us, the purely demonic nature of the country's leader made everyone pause. Again and again in the war with Iran, Saddam had shown that his desire for military victory and power had no moral limits. When he took prisoners, he tortured them. He shot many Iranian soldiers who were giving up under the white banner of surrender. He thought nothing of killing women and children or losing ten thousand men in a single battle. He even used poison gas on innocent people to put down a rebel uprising. It seemed that nothing would stand in his way in his quest to control an oil-rich strip of desert. He was a power-hungry egomaniac who seemed more than willing to use whatever cruel and immoral means possible to achieve his end. He appeared to have no conscience, no sense of morals, no compassion, and he seemed to care nothing for human life—not even the lives of his own people. And this was the man we were going to fight.

It was widely reported by sources inside Iraq as well as by Allied intelligence that Saddam not only ordered the executions of those who disagreed with his policies, but in some cases he actually called into his office those who dared to state a differing opinion and shot them himself. His tyranny was so great that his Arab neighbors would rather have Christians come and fight alongside them than allow Saddam to continue to rule in the region. Thus ironically, it was Saddam Hussein who opened the door of the Arab world to us. Many people who knew the area well, however, wondered if we had the intestinal fortitude to stand up to this madman and his henchmen.

In light of what we knew about Saddam and his methods, our main concern before the actual fighting began was not so much whether we could win a war, but what that victory would cost. How many of our people would die? In late fall, it was leaked that the military had already ordered almost 70,000 coffins. This news sobered a great number of people who were caught up in the strutting war-hero image of battle. These coffins were ordered by people who expected to use them—and they were not intended for enemy soldiers. They were for Americans. Did we as a nation have the kind of nerve and heart necessary for this kind of battle?

In World War II, Korea, and Vietnam, I held the hands of grown men who wept and moaned about going into combat. They were afraid that they would die. And I have known chaplains who were just as frightened. There is no way of judging how any of us will face that wall of death until we come to it, but it has been my experience that those who know and love the Lord are better at coping with thoughts of death than those who don't. Courage comes through faith, and faith comes from a living God.

Before the war, the talk I heard again and again from civilians concerned not so much the state of our soldiers' faith, but the beliefs of the Iraqi men. The understanding was that the enemy soldiers looked forward to dying in combat. The Iraqis thought that by facing their enemy, courageously fighting him, and then dying a glorious death, they would go straight to the highest level of heaven. It was said that they believed this so deeply that they prayed for the opportunity to live it out.

In World War II, Japan used kamikaze pilots. Since I was working in naval aviation at the time, I saw these crazed men gladly kill themselves for the cause of their homeland. And nothing started our men thinking about their own mortality faster than seeing someone gladly give up his life for a cause he believed in. Over and over again we asked ourselves why they were doing this. Such a desperate and devoted enemy may not have a chance of beating your army, but he stands a very good chance of killing a lot of your men.

And this was the kind of enemy that we feared in the Middle East. We didn't expect the Iraqis to hide. Instead, we expected them to face us boldly and fight fiercely. We didn't expect an easy victory, and we tried to prepare ourselves for a war that would be long, drawn out, and bloody.

For our men and women who were waiting on the front lines, these thoughts about the enemy and the fears they aroused were nearly impossible to forget.

Our soldiers were there, just miles from Iraq, and they were on alert. They knew all too well that they were the ones who would have to face Saddam on his own turf. They undoubtedly feared what might happen more than any of us can imagine. Theirs was a fear that often haunted their sleep and always followed them during the day. They were constantly preparing themselves for the battle, for fighting—if necessary—to the death.

Watching this kind of fear overtake people is a strange experience. The only way someone who has not been in combat can begin to comprehend the claustrophobic nature of terror is to imagine your own greatest fear. If you are afraid to fly, consider how you would feel if you were forced to fly all day and all night. Everyone else was allowed to get off the plane, but you had to stay on board. As the time dragged on, your pain and frustration would begin to overrule your logic. You would imagine the worst, your fear would grow, and you would eventually become irrational and unglued. In military language, you would crack. And what people feel during actual combat can be even worse.

Our chaplains saw these fears manifest themselves in a variety of ways. Some soldiers talked about family—recalling special moments, holiday traditions, the old homestead, Mom's special suppers, the way their kids looked forward to Christmas, even the day-to-day joys that are too easily taken for granted. As these soldiers talked, they never mentioned death or dying, but their every word seemed to scream, "I don't want to lose all that I now have!"

Other soldiers didn't talk at all. Although they might have four beautiful children, they would not speak of them. As they faced the possibility of combat, they seemed to be trying to forget all the reasons they had for living and to immerse themselves in a gloomy place that offered nothing but the shadow of death. They lived in a lonely, solitary world even though they were surrounded by thousands of Americans. They were prepared to advance on the enemy, but they had retreated inside themselves.

These reactions—talking around the fear and not talking at all—were not unusual. In the wars in which I served, I had seen soldiers react in much the same way. Men and women in the Persian Gulf were dealing with the same emotions that American soldiers dealt with in World War II, Korea, and Vietnam. Some soldiers deeply regretted things they had done, especially those things which had hurt people, while others lamented things they hadn't gotten to do. Some individuals reacted angrily to minor irritations, others cried, and still others seemed to be past caring about anything. It was as if these soldiers were already dead.

Yet, in the Persian Gulf War, unlike some of the earlier wars, something else was afoot—and that "something else" was the large number of men and women praying. To an even a greater degree than I'd seen in World War II, soldiers were attempting to get right with God. In facing death honestly rather than giving up or panicking, many people decided to do something. Knowing that they couldn't face the very real possibility of imminent death by themselves, they turned to the Lord.

The people I was dealing with on the home front were also searching for answers about how to handle death. They, too, were afraid that the Persian Gulf conflict would cost us the lives of tens of thousands of our youngest and best. Many Americans were worried that they would never see their loved ones again. With almost one in every fifty Americans either stationed in or en route to the Gulf, everybody knew somebody who was in harm's way. Consequently, death—that inevitability which most of us ignore, figuring that it will happen to us only when we are very old and "ready"—was hanging over the heads of millions every second of every day.

It may have taken the war to alert us to death's presence, but in reality death is always near us. Each year over twenty-six thousand Americans are killed by drunk drivers. But do we think about death when we get in the car to run an errand, go to church, pick up the kids from school, or go on vacation? No, we put it out of our minds because we are convinced that it can't happen to us. And what about all the innocent people killed in violent acts of crime or the misuse of firearms? Will that kind of death come to us? The answer most of us would give is a flat no.

We read statistics, hear about victims of a natural disaster, watch those around us battle disease, and go to funerals, but we rarely say, "There, but for the grace of God, go I." That simple statement, however, is profoundly true. Our military men and women realized that at any moment they could be called home, and so, too, we should realize that none of us is promised another tomorrow, another hour, even another minute. On the battlefield people were readying themselves for the possibility of death by getting things right with their Lord and Master. They recognized in a vivid and powerful way the preciousness of life, and most had come to realize how quickly this fragile gift could slip away. Many people on the home front weren't dealing with their mortality with as much realism and honesty. As it turned out, it would prove much safer to see action in the Gulf War than to drive our highways or walk the streets of our largest cities. That being the case, who was most in need of revival and prayer?

As I said in the preceding chapter, Chaplain David Plummer's words concerning the real enemy we were confronting overseas hit home with me. David counseled many of our men and women before they were deployed, and he answered a multitude of questions about life and death. Knowing that, I couldn't help but again reach for one of his papers (this one a transcription of a speech I heard him give) as I thought about all those who had to face the possibility of dying in battle. Now, as I read his remarks, I realized that the Americans who had stayed home needed to hear David's words as much as those who were on the front lines. The message about death which David shared means as much in times of peace as it does in times of war.

When I was asked to put together a few remarks about confronting our own mortality, I knew it was because Jim was aware of a situation I was recently involved in. So, before I actually get to the meat of the issue, allow me to share with you that story.

I was sponsoring a brand new chaplain at Fort Riley. He had heard from various sources, including the Chief's office, that new chaplains who had not finished Phase III of training would not be deployed to Saudi. Just prior to applying for active duty, this chaplain had carefully investigated the possibility of being deployed because he was a novice in the Army. He was scared and didn't want to get in over his head. He had only been to the basic training course, and he had not received any follow-up in the reserves. He hadn't even begun to learn the ropes, and he had never been to the field. He had not experienced the basic things that most of us take for granted, feel very confident in, and know as well as we know the backs of our hands.

Even though he knew he wasn't ready—and even though all of us would have agreed with that judgment—he was told in a telephone call that he should be ready for deployment to Saudi Arabia within two weeks. What a shock! He felt that it had to be a mistake. This was not the way it was supposed to work, and yet here was his assignment. Prepared or not, fully trained or not, he was on his way to a possible battle zone. Needless to say, this chaplain was very ill at ease about his duties, but he was also struggling with issues concerning his own mortality. Like many of our soldiers on the front, he was having problems dealing with death.

We all must consider the issue of our own mortality. This nervous chaplain is not alone. What he was confronting and fearing is something we all must confront and deal with. I think it is therefore very important to establish a biblical foundation on this subject.

As we make our way through the New Testament, notice that there does not seem to be a great emphasis on the saints' deaths. As I read Scripture and go over the stories describing the deaths of these born-again, Spirit-filled believers, nothing really strikes me as a lingering, mournful situation. There just does not seem to be a lot of long, melancholic, grief-laden accounts of their deaths.

We read of the stoning of Stephen, and he simply "cried with a loud voice, 'Lord, lay not this sin to their charge,'" and then "he fell asleep." (Acts 7:60) The stoning had to be painful, but he just said, "Lord Jesus, receive my Spirit." (Acts 7:59) In today's lingo, what he really said was "Here I come!," and he went directly to the Lord.

To honor an oath he had flippantly made, King Herod had John the Baptist beheaded. When Scripture records the sordid details which prompted the murder, it only says that John was beheaded. Of course it tells us that his head was presented to Herod, but there does not seem to be a mournful lingering on the thoughts and emotions surrounding his death. Neither his followers or Jesus dwelled on it. Matthew simply records, "And his disciples came, and took up his body, and buried it, and went and told Jesus." (Matthew 14:12) When Jesus learned of John's death, He seemed to want to withdraw to an isolated area with His apostles, but He was distracted by a multitude's need for physical and spiritual ministry. So much for a lengthy mourning period over John's death.

Similarly, when a would-be disciple asked the Lord to allow him to first bury his father before joining the itinerant band, Jesus responded, "Follow me; and let the [spiritually] dead bury their [physically] dead." (Matt. 8:22)

Clearly, God is much more concerned about how the saints are stewards of their energies and lives than about the details of their deaths. After all, only Christ's death has vicarious efficacy. So why morbidly dwell, agonize, and "sorrow . . . as others which have no hope?" (1 Thess. 4:13)

The New Testament also addresses the topic of fear of death. The Word states that the fear of death is a slavery of the devil. Specifically, Hebrews 2:14,15 states, "Forasmuch then as the children are partakers of flesh and blood, He also Himself likewise took part of the same; that through death He might destroy Him that had the power of death, that is, the devil; and deliver them who through fear of death were all their lifetime subject to bondage."

This is real bondage! This is genuine slavery! Accordingly, if a believer has such a fear, he or she needs to pray through it.

The Apostle Paul frequently exposed himself to death. In reading from Acts through Philemon, it almost seems as though he goes looking for it. He does not appear to fear death at all. He practices what he preaches. Much of his ministry was spent in prison, and it is recorded that at least five times he received thirty-nine lashes. He suffered a minimum of three beatings with rods, and he was stoned. He was also shipwrecked three times, once spending a night and a day on the open sea. He was a Christian who was constantly on the move, and as such he lived in danger of natural disasters, bandits, false brothers, and hostile Jews, Romans, and Gentiles. He was a man with a price on his head. He had to do without most of the basics a great deal of the time. And he had to feel a certain amount of stress concerning the welfare of all the churches he was so close to. Death was always all around him.

Still, Paul was not too concerned about his own mortality. It seems that something else was more pressing. In Philippians 1:15-26, we catch a view of his philosophy of life and death. While the entire passage can serve us as inspiration and motivation, four of the verses really jump out:

"For me to live is Christ, and to die is gain . . . . For I am in a strait betwixt the two, having a desire to depart, and to be with Christ; which is far better: Nevertheless to abide in the flesh is more needful for you. And having this confidence, I know that I shall abide and continue with you all for your furtherance and joy of the faith."

I have heard a prominent Christian say some things that seem to tie right in with Paul's message—"Hey, folks, heaven's not so bad after all!" and "Boy, I sure get homesick sometimes!"

Think about those two statements. If you do, you will find that they are true in Paul's case as well as our own. Paul was tired of being shipwrecked, stoned, beaten, and thrown in prison. He was being attacked by so many people that even he couldn't keep up with them. There couldn't have been much joy in being naked, cold, and starving. I am sure that this man of great faith longed for the

Lord to take him home. After all, he says, "If I go home, I'm going to be with the Lord, and that's better off by far!"

On the other hand, Paul realized that the Lord still had work for him to do. And even though life was a struggle, he accepted this load and did his work for the glory of the One he longed to be with. He was happy with his situation!

So, was Paul concerned about his death? No! He was actually more concerned about his life, and that is a great lesson for every Christian.

I am going to cut in on David's commentary for a moment and look more closely at how his words tie into what all of us must deal with—the fact that we are mortal and will die.

Some of us get so wrapped up in living that we ignore the importance of what we are doing with our lives. Men like Paul always seemed to have their purpose for living in clear focus. They knew that they were involved in the Lord's work, and they also knew that even if they were tired, there would be time to rest when Jesus called them home. Some of us, however, are so caught up in thoughts of dying that we fail to live. We become so worried that we will never get everything done—meet all our deadlines, reach all our goals, live out all our dreams—that we fail to do anything but worry. No person ever had any more to do than Paul, yet he never seemed to be in such a hurry that he became overly stressed and unable to function. Even though death was always around him, the pressure to get things done before he went to be with the Lord never clouded his vision.

I do not think that God is nearly as concerned about our death or our creature comforts as He is about our faithfulness to our mission in life. He is much more concerned about our obedience to the leading of His Spirit, our willingness to go where He sends us, and our efforts to do what He asks us to do. It is obedience that He is looking for; He looks for faithfulness and trust in Him. I think that this is the general principle which we need to examine and contemplate as we confront our own mortality.

And it is essential that we apply this principle to our own lives, that we confront mortality, that we put it directly in front of us—especially when circumstances are difficult.

I will readily admit to you that I have never seen combat. There have probably been times when I have come close to losing my life and didn't know it. But to stare into the face of certain death is something I do not know. Still, I have confronted my own mortality, and I have learned to live life with purpose.

Our brother and sister chaplains are facing the reality of death right now! They are experiencing situations—they are feeling, hearing, seeing, and smelling things—that most of us will never live. While they are learning to deal with the issue of death in a very real manner, we need to remember to pray for them, to encourage them, and to contemplate what they are going through. Isn't that what Paul requested of those to whom he wrote?

Let me go back to the situation I mentioned at the beginning. The chaplain I told you about had a horrible fear of death. Satan held this man in real bondage when it came to him facing his mortality. I wanted badly to minister to this man, so I met with him and his wife on several occasions.

I felt a bit awkward. After all, I couldn't tell him that I had been there. I hadn't. I didn't really know what he would be going through in a war situation. So, rather than try to comfort him in that manner, I shared with him this principle: don't focus on fear or the thoughts of how you could die; instead, focus on why God is putting you where He is. In other words, think about how you could live for God, not how you could die for Him.

We chaplains are expected to be well-prepared and highly-trained. Thus we are expected to have wonderful counseling skills. But how can we do our jobs and help others if we cannot deal with things ourselves?

People who do not know the Lord have a genuine right to be scared to death and scared of death. Can you imagine not having any hope of eternity? Imagine thinking that everything comes down to a battle in the sands of Saudi or a senseless car wreck on a lonely rural road. Imagine living as if, in that one brief moment, it is over forever!

We have to offer people who feel this way something that we know is there. We have to get into the hearts of all those who are bound by the fear of death—and we have to free them. These people need to hear the Good News of Jesus Christ.

We can tell them, "You may not be here tomorrow, but you can make yourself right with God today. Then you will know that you are going to spend eternity in heaven with the Lord." There is security in that knowledge. You can take comfort in that promise and have hope in it. God's gift of eternal life can bring you peace right now. But in order for us to share this Gospel message with others, we must live it as Paul did.

I cannot imagine the Lord telling Paul early in his ministry, "Paul, I have some wonderful things ahead of you. Your ministry will touch millions. Of course, you are going to be shipwrecked three times, and you'll spend a great deal of your life starving and thirsty floating in the open sea. You'll also be tortured, stoned, hated, and tossed in prison. Your friends will turn on you, you will have a price on your head, and most of the time you won't have good clothes, a warm bed, or enough to eat. Now, let's get started!"

Had the Lord told this to Paul, I am sure that even this great man would have had second thoughts. Our men and women in the Gulf will undoubtedly face hardships, yet we cannot dwell on this fact of war, this fact of life. Granted, hardships endured for a lost cause are worth nothing. And, unfortunately, this is how many people live their lives. They sell themselves out to causes that don't matter, and when they do face death, there is the feeling of being cheated.

We don't want the men and women we touch in life—be it on the battlefield or here at home—to feel as if they have been cheated when they face death. We want them to feel that everything they have endured is worth the price. And the only way we can make this knowledge a reality is to share with them the truth that Paul knew.

David's message—the honest words about the hard-to-face issue of death—must be at the center of any spiritual revival in our nation and the world. In the wars in which I have served my country, I have seen many men face death with the terror that comes from uncertainty.

During the Korean War, one of the most popular country tunes was a now familiar Gospel song "I Saw the Light." Hank Williams, a favorite of many of the G.I.'s, wrote and performed it, and many of the men used to sing the lyrics again and again. Yet, in a touch of irony, Hank Williams seemingly never understood the words he penned. Just weeks before his death he told another entertainer, "That's the problem—there just ain't no light!"

Right now millions of people are as much in the dark as the songwriter was at that moment. Hank was twenty-nine years old—about the same age as the men who were serving in the war and listening to his music—when he died of a heart attack. I am sure that he thought he was in far less danger of meeting death than the men in battle were. Yet most of them came home, safe and unhurt, and he died, young and alone in the back of a car. But knowing Paul's words, reading about Jesus' life, memorizing famous hymns, and even writing inspirational thoughts won't necessarily mean feeling secure in the shadow of death. We must really know and believe in Jesus—otherwise there "ain't no light!"

Remember the young alcoholic helped by one of our chaplains? He replaced his need for liquor with a love for the Spirit of Jesus. This man lost his need to drink because he no longer needed to run from the demons that had been chasing him before he found Jesus. He had lost his fears. He had confronted his own mortality and embraced Jesus.

It may have taken Saddam and the war to get many of us thinking about death, but it shouldn't have been so. Likewise, we shouldn't need to go to war before we consider the state of our salvation.

Each day we are involved in a battle for our eternal lives. Just as Saddam promised to bury us in the sand, the Devil himself has promised to take possession of our souls. So why do we wait to look at death before we look to Jesus? Why don't we see the present moment as a chance to find meaning in life and death?

When he sees death all around him, a combat soldier discovers that we do not own our lives. Life is a gift from God, and at some point He is going to ask us to give it back to Him. He didn't place us here to merely exist or to do the Devil's work. Rather, God wants us to respond to His will for our lives. If we do, He gives us the ultimate reward of forgiveness of sins, salvation, and eternal life.

Traditionally, revivals are thought of as times when preachers give their hottest hell-fire-and-brimstone messages. A revival is a time when the mission seems to be to "scare the hell" out of the lost. And why has revival almost always been approached this way? Because this seems to be the only method that effectively gets people to face their own mortality. It seems that people have to be able to breathe the smoke and feel the heat.

In the hot desert of Saudi—with its huge scorpions, unrelenting sun, endless miles of desolate sand, scorching winds, and shadows of war looming just beyond the horizon—men and women smelled the fire and felt the heat. When they heard Saddam's threats, they felt as though they had heard the voice of Satan. As they looked around at others who had no hope and no security and who were experiencing no love, they began to realize that a heavy dose of that "old-time religion" just might give them something to calm their spirits and quench their thirst. And so, by the tens of thousands, they turned to Jesus.

In their letters, they spoke of the peace they were finding and how, even though they were far away from their homes and families, they felt loved. Not only did these men and women find a sense of purpose for themselves in this war, they also found a sense of purpose for their lives. We are all at war, and it is time we all turned our lives over to God. Tomorrow may be too late!

CHAPTER EIGHT

Revival in A Land of Restrictions

"I want you to know God is working in so many ways here in Saudi Arabia. He continues to work in the hearts of those who will let Him enter in. We are in a land where just months ago you would be asked to leave for simply spreading the word of Christianity. Today thousands of Christians are here, speaking about Christ and the blood He shed for our sins.

"I've never been so content with what I am doing. The Lord is using me with a real spirit of compassion for His soldiers. I love them all.

"Let me tell you, whatever the end result, God truly has been here by my side, never forsaking me."

Sgt. Timothy Page, Christian layman in Saudi Arabia
—November 1990

THE WORDS OF SGT. TIMOTHY PAGE WERE A CONFIRmation of the miracles taking place in the deserts of the Persian Gulf during Operation Desert Shield. We had been invited to a land where Christianity is forbidden by law, we had overcome huge obstacles and restrictions placed upon us by the host nation and our own government, and we had seen a spiritual revival begin in a place where the displaying of a cross is illegal, to the extent that the Red Cross must be called the Red Crescent. Thousands of bandages were returned to be relabeled because they had red crosses on them.

The nation of Saudi Arabia is in a unique position in the Islamic world. The religion's two holiest places are within its boundaries, and the nation is ruled by the strictest Islamic laws. Notably, Saudi leaders have never shown any flexibility regarding those laws. Consequently, the arrival of an army of non-Islamic men and women was a move that few could have predicted.

To put this event into perspective, consider that a TV antenna on the roofs of buildings in Saudi is not allowed to have a horizontal bar for fear that someone might mistake it for a cross. All Bibles, Christian books, and Christian literature are banned. To own any of these materials is against the law and can mean prison time. The punishment for converting from Islam to Christianity is having both hands cut off. As a result of this persecution, the Christians who live in the nation are, by necessity, members of underground churches. They have secret knocks and special hand signals, and they practice hiding all religious symbols in case of a government raid. Believers in Saudi are even more oppressed than Christians in China.

In an effort to make sure that our troops didn't upset the Islamic order of Saudi, special orders were issued to all men and women as they pulled out from their home bases. These instructions, for instance, specified that chaplains would be referred to as "morale officers" and would not be allowed to wear their insignias, crosses, or Stars of David on their uniforms. All worship services would be closed to the media and held out of sight of any Saudi citizens. Religious materials were for U.S. personnel only and must either be stored or trashed if they were not being used behind the prescribed closed doors. No Christian music was allowed to be played in public, nor was anyone to pray where the news media or local citizens would be able to witness the activity. After receiving these orders and being reminded again and again about the restrictions, the soldiers were then told that they could freely worship within these bounds. Many wondered, "Where? And how?"

When word got out that we would be welcomed in the Persian Gulf to rescue and protect the host nations but that we could not practice the most fundamental of our religious beliefs, Americans spoke up. When the basic liberties of U.S. soldiers were being denied, people made noise, wrote letters, and began to lobby for change. I was one of the most vocal.

John Whitehead, president of the Rutherford Institute, launched a congressional investigation into the matter, and he threatened a lawsuit. Newspapers, magazines, and television newscasts—brought to you by the same folks who normally ignore matters of religion—got involved too. As the reporting continued and the debates raged, things were happening in Saudi in spite of the restrictions.

The Chaplaincy of Full Gospel Churches—thanks to private citizens as well as the ministries of Larry Lea, Jimmy Hester, Dick Bontke of the Arlington Christian Center, Ken Copeland, Richard Roberts, Merlin Caruthers, Ed Cole Ministries, End Time Handmaidens, and Worship International— sent over 150,000 crosses, 300,000 Christian tapes, and boxes of Bibles and other Christian materials. These items not only got through, but they were distributed quickly throughout the region. Other individuals and churches were involved in similar programs. The Good News was getting out!

As Chaplain Jeff Houston, a Baptist minister with the 82nd Airborne, noted, "Desert Shield troops are praying, witnessing, and being baptized in record numbers. Christians have begun to stand out like beacons and have become a rallying point for soldiers." Houston's words were picked up and printed in the *Los Angeles Times*. The secular media was suddenly concerned about winning souls to Christ. Was it that big a news item? If it was, brothers and sisters, then we were seeing a real miracle in the Gulf!

Desert Shield Command Chaplain David Peterson said, "There is a spiritual hunger [here] like I have never seen." Added Chaplain Clifford Weathers, "Chapel attendance is at an all-time high." Both men pointed to the Saudis' ban on alcohol and pornography as reasons why men were sobering up and searching for the Lord. Even during the early days of deployment, some Bible studies were going on for as long as eight hours. There was a hunger like I had never experienced in any war I'd served in.

The Boston Globe, reporting on the spiritual

viewpoint of the soldiers, pointed out that the situation overseas was similar to that in another era. Colin Nickerson said it this way: "Religious military men and women in Saudi Arabia find their situation somewhat akin to that of early Christians in Roman times. They practice their faith almost covertly, well away from Arab eyes. But worship they do, despite the nervousness of the U.S. command and occasional rumbles from conservative Islamic clerics, who are a politically potent force in Saudi society." Keep in mind that this report is not from one of our chaplains. Neither is it from a religious publication. This story and hundreds of others like it appeared in secular newspapers across the country.

Nickerson's article—as well as stories by AP, UPI, CNN, ABC, NBC, and CBS—pointed out the triumph as well as the frustration felt by Americans and the more than seven hundred chaplains stationed in the Gulf. A Navy chaplain told a newspaperman, "We are morale officers who are permitted to hold fellowship meetings. Apparently morale and fellowship are okay with the Saudis." Marine Corps chaplain Stan Scott pointed out, "The concessions the Saudis have made in allowing me to serve my clerical duties here are phenomenal."

At one point, a Saudi Ministry of Information officer admitted, "Americans have generously come to the defense of our kingdom, so it would be ungenerous for us to interpret our law too narrowly during this crisis." Most soldiers agreed, feeling strongly that they should be allowed to display symbols of their faith, pray in public, and openly talk about their beliefs. But when men and women saw these doors closed to them, they learned just how precious freedom of worship really is. They also realized the value of the faith that this freedom of worship protects. By trying to silence and hide Christianity, the Islamic restrictions actually sharpened the hunger for faith and planted seeds for revival. In trying to deny spiritual food to American believers, the Saudis made our men and women much more hungry for it!

As one Navy paramedic said, "I'm not a troublemaker and I don't want to offend Moslems or anyone else. It just seems wrong to me that Americans who have come to defend the Arabs should be asked to sacrifice our traditions and beliefs." In other words, his faith—like the faith of many other soldiers—meant more to him than anything else and he wanted to live it!

This "stand up and be counted" kind of faith kept chaplains busy trying to fill requests for Bible studies and religious services. A Methodist chaplain reported, "I can't tell you exactly where I am or how many of us there are, but I can say that the body of Christ and the Spirit of God are alive and well here. I've run out of Bibles, I've run out of worship space, and I've run out of ice. One airman wants to be baptized by immersion, but I'm having a hard time finding anything with enough water in it. These are wonderful problems to have!"

Lt. Col. Carlton L. Harper of the 101st Airborne Division wrote to me, "I know I can count on your prayers and support in proclaiming the Gospel to my soldiers who are more open now than I have ever seen in my military ministry."

Still, the need for even greater religious freedom remained. Tents sprang up everywhere and were turned into "Canvas Cathedrals," but men and women had trouble finding them. Chaplains were not allowed to hand out fliers telling of worship times and locations, nor were they able to put up a cross or any other symbol to indicate that this tent was a house of worship. Being forced to hide their faith soon began to irritate many of the soldiers.

Chaplain Jim Agnew wrote me, "When the Saudis didn't want women driving or in positions of authority, our government told them that if they wanted our army, they had to take the women as well. So why can't the Saudis be told that our soldiers have a right to practice their faith and that our chaplains are going to support that right? Our newspaper has been edited to take out any reference to anything biblical, and chaplains are referred to as 'morale support officers.' We have been told if we are conducting a service and the media comes by, to stop worshiping until they leave. It is getting ridiculous. . . I hope that something can be done soon so we can minister openly to soldiers without concern for who is watching."

In spite of these limitations, Jim found a way to reach hundreds. In another of his letters, he said, "I just had to write to tell you of the tremendous growth in worship services—468 people in two services just yesterday. There are many Full Gospel service men and women over here. As the days go on, we see more and more needs and more and more soldiers seeking assistance. The Lord has granted me favor with both the command and the soldiers, and this has opened the door for my ministry."

I couldn't help but marvel at the news. Here we were, being restricted in ways that none of us had ever experienced, but still saving lost souls for Christ. Not only were our chaplains having a tremendous response, but chaplains from other denominations were, too. The reports which came across my desk were filled with statistics and enthusiasm: "Fourteen saved today, ten rededications. . ." "Twenty-three came to Christ just tonight . . ." "Men and women are out witnessing and sharing the Gospel. I've never seen anything like it." "This is the most exciting time in my life. God is alive and working miracles."

In my letters to congressmen, I noted that in 1853 Commodore Perry of the U.S. Navy became fully accepted by the Japanese emperor when Perry refused to meet the emperor during Perry's time of Sunday worship. The emperor postponed the meeting until the next day and said that Perry could be trusted because he was faithful to his God. This trust opened the door to the Orient for the United States. We needed to demand the same kind of rights now!

With thousands of people being saved, I wondered what could be accomplished if we didn't have the burden of heavy restrictions on our chaplains. How many other soldiers would feel the power of

Jesus' hand? How many more would come under the conviction of the Spirit? How many would be healed in heart and body? And how many would be given the special gifts of the Holy Spirit? We simply couldn't let this opportunity for revival slip by. Something had to be done. I wanted action, and our country did, too. As I fought to get changes made, I was thankful that our military people serving at sea didn't have to bow to the edicts of an Islamic government. In the Navy, the men and women were as free to worship as they were at home, and they were seeking the Spirit.

Lt. Robert Duane Purser of the *USS Worden* wrote me, "I'm having a wonderful time of ministry. I have a radio show on Sunday afternoon and a daily TV show called 'Rap with the Chap,' and they have caught on like wildfire. Some of the guys wrote a memo to the captain asking for more time for the show. Currently it is approximately fifteen to twenty minutes long. On Wednesday afternoon we have a praise and worship service in the C.O.'s cabin!"

Reports from other Navy ships indicated the same kind of interest in God's Word, and commanders were often leading the way. The two major problems that our chaplains seemed to have were inadequate space for all who wanted to attend services and not enough hours in the day to answer all the requests for one-on-one visits. The Spirit of the Lord was blowing mightily across the seas.

On the home front we were also receiving spiritual leadership from our elected officials. The President and many Congressional leaders were calling on the nation to seek God's guidance and protection in the Persian Gulf situation. On the floor of both Houses, the name of the Lord was repeated again and again. The longer the military build-up went on, the more evident the need for Divine intervention became. Finally, on November 2, 1990, President George Bush issued the following proclamation.

Throughout American history, the people of this Nation have depended on Almighty God for guidance and wisdom. Both Scripture and experience confirm that the Lord hears the prayers of those who place their trust in Him. Time and again, in peril and uncertainty, doubt and decision, we Americans have turned to God in prayer and, in so doing, found strength and direction.

Today the United States and, indeed, all civilized countries are being challenged by a dictator who would brazenly deny the sovereignty of other nations in order to achieve regional hegemony and to wield undue influence over the global economy. Iraqi forces continue to occupy neighboring Kuwait, terrorizing that nation's citizens in an affront to international law and fundamental standards of morality. Scores of U.S. civilians and citizens of other nations continue to be held hostage under inhuman conditions in both Kuwait and Iraq. To deter further aggression, thousands of American service men and women have been deployed and remain on duty in the demanding climate of the Persian Gulf region. They, too, face considerable hardship and danger. We are grateful for the loyalty, devotion to duty, and sacrifices of the members of our Armed Forces. Yet we know that military strength alone cannot save a nation or bring it prosperity and peace; as the Scriptural writer speaks, "Unless the Lord watches over the city, the watchman stays awake in vain." With these grave concerns before us, we do well to recall as a Nation the power of faith and the efficacy of prayer.

The Psalmist proclaimed: "God is our refuge and strength, a very present help in our trouble." Today let us turn to Him, both as individuals and as a Nation, to ask for His continued mercy and guidance. Let us pray for peace in the Persian Gulf, and let us ask the Lord to protect all those Americans and citizens of other nations who are working to uphold the universal cause of freedom and justice half a world away from home. May it please the Lord to grant all leaders of nations involved in this crisis the wisdom and courage to work towards its just and speedy resolution.

The Congress, by House and Joint Resolution 673, has authorized and requested the President to issue a proclamation designating November 2, 1990, as a National Day of Prayer.

NOW, THEREFORE, I, GEORGE BUSH, president of the United States of America, do hereby proclaim November 2, 1990, as a National Day of Prayer for American service personnel and American civilians stationed or held hostage in the Persian Gulf region. I urge all Americans to pause on this day to pray for these individuals and their families. I ask that prayer be made for commanders of American military forces in the region and leaders in other nations that have deployed military forces in the Middle East to stop this aggression. I also urge the American people and their elected representatives to give thanks to God for His mercy and goodness and humbly to ask for His continued help and guidance in all our endeavors.

IN WITNESS WHEREOF, I have hereunto set my hand this second day of November, in the year of our Lord nineteen hundred and ninety, and of the Independence of the United States of America the two hundred and fifteenth.

With this proclamation added to the already growing interest in returning to the foundations of faith, the spiritual movement on the home front was really taking hold. People wanted to believe that their prayers could stop a madman from following through on his threats. The Thanksgiving holiday was approaching and, despite our hopes for peace, war was looking more and more likely. At the time of year when we give thanks for our blessings and look forward to the season of peace on earth, hundreds of thousands of Americans were separated from family and friends because of a maniac's desire for power. We as a nation had a great deal to think about this Thanksgiving season.

Pastors and church leaders from all denominations let me know that they were seeing what I, too, was seeing: more than at any other time in recent history, people were going back to church. Just like the tents our chaplains were worshiping in overseas, our Sunday schools, sanctuaries, and chapels didn't seem to have enough room for all those wishing to "come back home."

God—the same God whom many of these men and women had taken for granted and ignored—was being sought after, found, and worshiped again. The reasons were quite basic. We were scared, we had been reminded of death, we felt unable to control the situation in the Gulf, and we needed something or Someone on which we could lean. Our burdens were simply too heavy to carry by ourselves.

Anyone coming to the Lord's house who hasn't been there in a long time excites those of us who preach and share the Word, but it is especially sweet when families attend services together. And we were seeing a large number of families come to church. As one of my friends noted, "Every Sunday is like Christmas and Easter." Parents were once again taking their children to church.

Not only were people coming to church, but they were also praying. In a national poll, almost fifty percent of the Americans interviewed said that they pray on a daily basis. It had been fifty years since so many had freely admitted a constant communication with their Lord. What our chaplains in the Gulf were reporting, our pastors at home were seeing, too—a revival had begun on both sides of the globe.

As the Christmas season grew closer, the letters I received from overseas indicated that more and more men and women were being bold witnesses for Christ. Soldiers were carrying their Bibles in plain sight and proudly displaying the crosses we had sent them. It was not unusual to see men and women praying in public, as well as openly talking about their faith. As they prepared to stand up to Saddam, our people were also making a stand for Christ! This was especially evident to Chaplain Jim Agnew on Thanksgiving Day.

Jim had just finished conducting services and was visiting with soldiers within the confines of the "out-of-sight but never out-of-mind chapel" when he was told about an accident. A man in the transport division had wrecked a truck. He was badly injured, the vehicle was mangled, and even though all possible equipment was being used, those working were having little success freeing him from the wreck. By the time Jim arrived on the scene, the man had been trapped for over four hours.

Since the accident had happened on a public road off the base, a large crowd of both service personnel and local citizens had gathered. For a moment, Jim hesitated outside the group. He wondered if ministering to the needs of this man would constitute a violation of U.S./Saudi restrictions concerning religious conduct. Saying a short prayer, he reached to remove his cross, but then he stopped. A power came over him, and he realized that he must wear his cross as he did his duty as a chaplain.

Jumping out of his truck, he ran up to the crowd and made his way through it. As he looked down on the badly injured man, Jim saw the pain etched all over the young soldier's face. Jim also noticed a certain hopelessness hanging in the air. It was Thanksgiving Day, and this poor man, half a world away from home and family, was trapped in a truck in the middle of the desert. Everything around him, except those trying to get him out of the truck, was foreign to him. Then he looked up and saw Jim.

"Chaplain!" he exclaimed, a sparkle showing in his eyes.

"Yes," Jim softly answered.

"Thank God you are here," he sighed, "and thank God I'm still alive."

"Do you want me to pray?" Jim asked as he leaned close to the trapped man.

"Please," he pleaded.

In front of a crowd of Muslims, and in spite of restrictions that forbade him to do so, Jim fell to his knees and began to pray out loud. Many of the Americans gathered and prayed with him. For the first time in their lives, this group of Saudis was witnessing the practice of another religion. They saw firsthand a man calmed by the presence of God. They watched another man read from a Bible. They heard God's Word.

Neither Jim nor I know what these Muslim observers thought. All we know is that they were moved to silence as the prayer and reading took place. I am sure that these Saudis talked about what they had seen. Even after the soldier was freed from the wreckage and air-lifted out and the Americans returned to their stations, the local citizens stayed at the scene. Could this have been a seed planted, the beginning of these men coming to know the Lord?

On December 1, another of our men reported, "While training up north during the past month, we held services four to five times a week for each of the line companies. Several of the first sergeants have received Christ. In turn, they have led their soldiers to Christ and have brought them to the services. In just one service, twelve of these men came to know Jesus. Out here, every day is Sunday. Our Bible studies are growing. We can't fit them into one tent anymore! What a great problem! So many of these soldiers are hungry for the Word!"

In the sands, at sea, on ships, in tanks, on trucks, in tents, and of course in chapel, chaplains and converts alike were sharing the Gospel. Restrictions or not, the words of Jesus Christ were being spoken more and more! Men and women were being overcome by the Spirit, and, in the middle of a potential war zone, tens of thousands of soldiers were singing, praising the Lord, and reading their Bibles.

Officers were actually running to our chaplains and bragging about how many men in their unit they had brought to Jesus. Others were coming to us crying and speaking in tongues. They were awed, confused, and deeply moved.

Between Thanksgiving and Christmas, many more service men and women turned to the Lord. Part of the reason was that they couldn't be home for the holidays, and this fact forced them to look at just how lonely their lives really were. For thousands of soldiers who had no family and no one waiting at home—no one writing or sending presents—this time was especially hard. It was bad enough being a thousand miles away from home, but to be so far away from home and have no one care was very tough. In the words of an old song, "Where could I go but to the Lord?"

The separation during the holiday season was equally tough on those who did have families waiting for them. Some of these people opened gifts which reminded them how much they were missing and how much they were missed. Other soldiers knew that the cards and gifts loved ones had sent were being delayed due to logistics problems created by trying to deliver over two hundred tons of mail per day to five hundred thousand people spread over a huge area. It was a depressing time, and yet there was also something very special about it.

Our chaplains reported that many in their flock found Christmas very meaningful because they were so close to the area where Jesus was born and the countryside where He ministered. Other chaplains reported that men and women were touched by the specialness of celebrating a Christian holiday in the middle of the Islamic world. The hidden trees, the hymns sung behind walls of canvas, the meals and stories shared with those who had become their closest friends—all this made Christmas 1990 something that the soldiers would never forget. Missing the worship services, the TV specials, the music, the shopping, and the family times taught each of them that they would never again take such moments for granted.

Our chaplains also witnessed the precious beauty of all the Lord's people—representing a wealth of different backgrounds, races, cultures, and denominations—celebrating together the birth of Christ like a real family of God. Under clear skies and a canopy of stars that proclaimed the beauty and majesty of God's work, the true meaning of Jesus' birth was not lost in the noise of commercialism. Rather, Christmas was observed and experienced as the spiritual moment it is meant to be.

These men and women weren't looking for Santa; they were looking to the Lord.

Many of our chaplains sought out those who had received nothing from home during the holiday season and handed them a Bible. Thousands enthusiastically expressed their thanks, and many cried as they told the giver, "This is the only gift I got this year. I can't tell you how much it means to me."

Some of those Bibles will probably become a part of every Christmas celebration these men and women experience from now on. Every time they touch it, they will remember a chaplain, a moment in the desert or at sea, a time when God reached down with love to warm a lonely night. When many of these lost men and women read the Book, they found the power and real meaning of salvation.

As the Christmas season passed, the reality of the January 15 deadline for Saddam to get out of Kuwait began to loom very large in the minds of everyone. We were grateful that he had released all the foreign hostages (though he had done it more in an effort to win world favor than out of any real compassion), and we began to realize that he wasn't going to back down. He was going to make us fight.

As the countdown to war began, even more men and women joined in what was becoming a massive procession to God's altar of grace. By this time, several different sources estimated that more than twenty-five percent of those stationed in the Gulf had come to know the Lord—and this statistic doesn't take into account the huge number of Christians who knew Jesus before being deployed. In the military, it seemed, being a Christian was "in," and this kind of thinking was revolutionary. As one Christian officer observed, "By the time war is scheduled to begin, it might really be 'Onward Christian Soldiers!' Let's see Saddam stop that kind of power!"

Lt. R. Duane Purser of the *USS Worden* reported in early January that the Spirit was moving in a way he had never seen. Even when the ship was at liberty, things were happening. "Dear friends," Purser wrote, "Liberty ports have been interesting, especially Dubai, Abu Dhabi [United Arab Emirates], and Mina Sulman [Bahrain]. In Abu Dhabi, I took the men's choir to the international school, and we sang Christmas carols and gave testimonies to some three hundred students! Someone sent me a New Testament in parallel English and Arabic called the 'Blood of Life.' When we hit Bahrain the next time, I'm going to try and give it to a local. I'm learning some Arabic and can say the basics: 'Hello. How are you. Do you know God?' Ha! It throws them when you can speak their language a little because most Westerners don't take the time to try. They enjoy it when you attempt Arabic—it's a natural icebreaker!

"My ministry continues to be fruitful, even more now because everyone has built up an endurance for the stress and has more energy for Bible study. The other day something happened that was pretty neat. One of the sailors that I gave a book to was baptized in the Spirit as he was ironing his uniform in the laundry! With tears running down his cheeks, he related to me the story of his new life in the Spirit."

As our chaplains shared the Gospel with more and more of their soldiers and shipmates, the effects of these conversions were felt by others. Chaplain Skip Stanley wrote me about a sharing of the Spirit: "We have organized lay ministries to provide Bible studies for men who cannot come to the ones we conduct. The response to these has been overwhelming. Our laymen, some of them new Christians, have had six conversions just this week! We are so pleased and encouraged by what the Lord is doing!"

Ed Ahl, whose wife was doing such a great job on the home front, was amazed by the tremendous number of requests he was getting to share Jesus with his men. His official title in Saudi may have been "morale officer," but his message was reaching into the souls of both men and women. Ed wrote to me, "The ministry here is in great demand. The soldiers are scared, and a lot of them are turning to Jesus through salvation and rededication. This is great!"

Like so many others, Ed couldn't keep up with all those who were making serious commitments to the Lord. Others also were noting the revival that was going on. Lt. Col. Herbert Wheeler, USAF pilot, wrote me to share his insights into what was happening: "The nights are really beautiful here, especially when the moon is full, like it has been the last few nights. It's a reminder to me that God made this place also and gave it a special beauty of its own. I learned a long time ago that regardless of where we are, God's presence is always there—and the Saudi desert is no exception. It's wonderful to know that even here His love and blessings abound. The Holy Spirit has been moving in the camp as spiritual matters become more important to the men and women here. PRAISE THE LORD! See, He has a purpose for everything. These men and women may never have considered Christ had they not been brought here. I wouldn't be a bit surprised if this isn't happening at other bases as well. In fact, I believe that this may be an opening for Christianity in this region of the world, should the Lord tarry for the next generation or so."

Lt. Col. Wheeler was right. What he was seeing at his base was happening all across the Gulf on both land and sea. In some units, every man and woman was attending some type of service at least once a week. When Chief Michael Brown wrote me, he was more excited than I had ever known him to be. In the midst of war, he was experiencing a spiritual high!

He wrote: "We have seen souls saved and reclaimed to Christ during this deployment. The number attending our worship services has increased from five at the beginning to an average of over thirty now. This alone brings new meaning to the Scripture, 'He prepares a table before me in the presence of my enemies.' By the grace of God and the support of the many churches that we have in C.F.G.C., the ministry here continues to prosper. We have received books, tapes, cards, numerous letters, and other supplies from churches, church members, and various organizations. I have tried to respond to each letter personally, but there is just not enough time. I can't tell you what a blessing this is!"

Chaplain Skip Stanley echoed Michael's enthusiasm: "I have coordinated Catholic services for my battalion and provided Protestant services too. I have done a great deal of stress and religious counseling. Since coming to Saudi, I have had at least sixty-five professions of faith. Perhaps more! We have received wonderful support from so many churches. We are preparing for the ground assault now. It looks like it may be very intense. Pray for strength for us all!"

Certified Lay Leader Arnold Lewis told me, "I have been sharing tapes with members in the Gulf. This week I have learned that one of the members used the tapes together with personal ministry and led a young soldier to the Lord. The soldier was so excited that he called his mother, witnessed to her, and she accepted the Lord. Now they both are looking forward to witnessing to the rest of the family!"

So, in the middle of the Islamic Holy Land, in a place where strict laws attempted to keep the Gospel of Jesus Christ under wraps, God was reaching out and saving souls. At the same time His Word was claiming the lost in the United States as well. The fact that the Spirit was touching hearts on both sides of the world may have been the most remarkable thing about the growing revival. The power of faith and prayer was breaking down walls, working miracles, and changing the lives of men and women from all walks of life.

The prayers that were being prayed, the faith that was being lived, the Gospel that was being shared—these had real power, and that power offered a spiritual shield during the days and nights of Operation Desert Shield. It would be during Desert Storm, though, that this power would really break forth. It was then that the world would see the power not only of the United States, but of our Lord!

CHAPTER NINE

The Power of Prayer

A Marine's Last Prayer

Look, God, I've never spoken to you before. You see, God, they told me that you didn't exist, and like a fool I believed them.

Last night, out here in this sandbox, I saw you and I figured right then that they have lied to me. Had I taken time to see things that you've made, I would know they weren't calling a spade a spade.

It's funny, I had to come to this big sandbox before I took time to see the beauty of your face.

Well, I guess there isn't much more to say, but God, I'm sure glad I met you. I reckon the zero hour will be here any day now, but I'm not afraid since I know you're near.

Well, God, I've got to go. I really like you a lot; this I want you to know.

This fight will be horrible. Who knows, I may come home tonight. Even though I wasn't friendly to you before, I wonder God if you will wait for me at the gate?

Well, I have to go now.

P.S. It seems strange. Since I've met you, I'm not afraid to die.

From *The Navy Times*—January 21, 1991

JANUARY 15, THE DEADLINE SET BY THE UNITED NA-
tions for Iraq to withdraw from Kuwait, passed and
Saddam still showed no signs of backing down. All
across the United States, people feared the worst
and prayed for a miracle. Many were convinced that
a bloodbath was coming and that many of our soldiers would meet their Maker in the desert sands.

With the clock ticking, President George Bush,
an Episcopalian, called Bishop Edmond Browing on
the phone. They prayed together. Then the President called Senate Chaplain Richard Halverson.
They, too, prayed for peace.

The next morning, the President called one of
the nation's best known and most respected men of
God, Reverend Billy Graham. The President's message: "I need you!" Reverend Graham hurried to the
Oval Office. He arrived at 5:45 p.m. just as U.S.
bombers were nearing Baghdad.

The President, his advisers, and Reverend Graham watched television as the news bulletin appeared on the screen. Silent prayers were offered and
very little was said aloud as the men—joined by
Mrs. Bush—watched the reports of the raids. Later,
they dined.

At five different times during the evening, the
President asked Reverend Graham to pray. At one
point, the two men retired to a private room so they
could pray alone. After spending the night at the
White House, Reverend Graham led a worship ser-

vice in the Memorial Chapel at Fort Myer. Members of the White House staff, General Colin Powell, and the top military brass in Washington were present.

The prayers that day touched on the themes of understanding, guidance, and peace. One request stood out above all others: "Please grant quick success to this nation's just and right cause." In his twenty-minute message, Reverend Graham quoted Abraham Lincoln: "We will be on God's side." The service concluded with a final prayer and everyone sang "Amazing Grace." Before leaving Washington, Reverend Graham returned to the White House and once more joined the President in a time of prayer.

President Bush then summoned leaders of Congress to join him at a White House meeting. There he observed, "There's a lot of prayer going on here, on Capitol Hill, and across the whole country. And it will be that way until this war is over."

President Bush's leadership and his desire to seek the Lord in the worst of times showed his deep concern for our men and women in the Gulf. As Operation Desert Storm began—an operation that would mean destruction and death—the leader of the United States was attempting to strengthen the bridge of faith between the American people and their God. As the bombs fell, he was seeking a miracle.

Throughout the United States, men and women were praying for a miracle. A solemn mood had fallen over the country, and no matter where you were, you felt this deep concern. At sporting events, concerts, business meetings, homes, and of course churches, millions of people were going before the Lord's throne with heartfelt prayer. The actual start of the war had humbled us and sharply reminded us how little control we have over our lives. Who but Jesus had the answers to the questions which arise when death is imminent?

On the other side of the world, thousands of soldiers—some leading the air offensive and others busy preparing for ground warfare—were praying, too. Chaplains and commanders were leading their men in prayer over loudspeakers and in one-on-one meetings. The preparation for war may have been over for some, but the preparation of souls was still going on.

Before the actual outbreak of hostilities, a chaplain's job had been important, but now it was vital. The person leading the spiritual battle was key to how a unit would perform. If that chaplain did not have the deep faith which would enable him to lead, or if that chaplain was afraid, then the unit could face problems in combat. The soldiers would reflect the chaplain, either his strength or his weakness, his confidence or his fear.

So another dimension was added to our chaplains' already heavy loads: now they must not only show strength in prayer and witness, but in living under the shadow of death as well.

Chaplain Klon K. Kitchen, Jr., was a lieutenant stationed on the *USS Sylvania*. I knew him to be a man of deep convictions, a sure heart, and a loving hand, and I thought he would be an effective leader. When the war broke out, my confidence in Klon was confirmed. When his commanding officer filed a report on all his officers, the section dealing with Chaplain Kitchen was forwarded to me:

Chaplain Kitchen's performance has been outstanding. Though only here a short time, he has inspired the religious program to new levels. A dynamic, innovative officer, he has proven to be flexible and proficient under pressure. Chaplain Kitchen has quickly become my trusted adviser in all areas and has developed a warm rapport with all levels of command. A partial list of accomplishments includes:

- Received a Navy Achievement Medal, Gold star in lieu of Second Award, for his previous work with Navcomsta, Puerto Rico.
- After being on board for only two days, he joined us for a two-week cruise where he performed his duties with the poise of a seasoned crew member.
- Provided religious services and counseling and facilitated all religious needs on board.
- Handled the delivery of Amcross messages with the utmost care and proficiency. Sensitivity is his greatest asset.
- As department head, he took an already great department and improved its efficiency and usefulness to the command.
- Completed career information and counseling course for supervisors at Comluggru Two.

Chaplain Kitchen demonstrated superior performance as a Naval Officer. His untiring efforts, unfailing good judgment, effectiveness, and total devotion to duty seem unlimited. A team player who routinely operates far beyond the average lieutenant, Chaplain Kitchen has unlimited potential and my complete confidence. Extremely dependable, mature, productive, and professional, Lt. Kitchen has earned my strongest recommendation for accelerated promotion well ahead of his contemporaries.

Chaplain Kitchen is obviously a stellar example of the kind of chaplain we were sending to the Gulf. His commanding officer as well as his men seemed to regard him as more than a preacher. He was evidently the kind of man they wanted at their side in times of battle and in times of peace. He was a friend, a role model, a rock.

A few days after getting the Navy's official report, I received an update from Klon himself. The body of notes he sent revealed those qualities which had so impressed his commander. What he wrote to me was meant to apply strictly to his duty on the *Sylvania*, but his words can be heeded by every believer who is interested in living for Christ.

The Sunday service is really a very small part of what a chaplain does. Like in all things, what you live speaks more loudly than your words. My earlier letters told you a great deal about our ship and its schedule, but through it all, living the love of Jesus is the most important thing we do. A good chaplain is involved in all aspects of his command. In many cases, I've moved boxes with the men, stayed up all hours when they worked, and played with them when they played. This does not keep a chaplain from the responsibility of the services, but adds to that—to live a life before man that is pleasing in God's sight. . . A good chaplain realizes that strength comes from the Lord and that we live our lives unto Him.

War makes people remember they are mortals. It does not seem rational that something as heavy and large as this ship should float. Being at sea has a tendency to make one think about the possibility of meeting one's Maker. Being at sea also allows you to see the beauty of God and to hear and see His wonders in ways that you have never seen them before.

Add to this mix the war. The constant sound of missiles firing and planes taking off and landing has a way of putting everything into perspective. God has allowed and called chaplains to this work, to be available for those who are not sure how to talk with Him, to be available to those who know Him and to those who wish to.

Chaplains are here not only for the troops, but equally for the commanders of those troops. These men feel the responsibilities and their tremendous weight. Having a good relationship with your commanding officer is as important as anything else. It is your relationship with the CO that determines whether or not you have his support for the work you want to do for the Lord. Also, the chaplain can be the one person whom the CO can show his emotions to. This helps the CO as well as the troops by allowing the CO time to be a per-

son too. I thank God for the relationship I have
with my CO and for the support I get in the work
that is to be done.

God has called me to this position, and He
proves daily that He equips those who have been
called. But for His strength, I would have quit a
long time ago; but with His strength, I can do all
things—from lifting boxes to being a Naval Officer to being a chaplain. The most important thing
is to seek God's guidance and then do His will.
Availability is the key word. A chaplain needs to
be out of his office and where the troops are so
that, when they need him, he is right there.

What would the state of churches be if all of our
nation's pastors felt as strongly about their mission?
How many of them are working beside their flocks,
readily showing concern and compassion? How
many of them are respected for what they give
rather than simply because of their titles?

At the same time, don't the principles which
Chaplain Kitchen lives by apply just as well to any
lay Christian? Klon first earned the respect of his
shipmates and superiors by going the extra mile as
a Navy man. Having come to respect the chaplain,
they then allowed him into their lives. They also noticed his life-style. He therefore witnessed in every
facet of his life. Couldn't everyone who works in the
"real" world do this? Aren't hard workers—those
folks who go the extra mile—the ones whom people
turn to and depend on when they have problems?
Conscientiousness in the work place can become a

real testimony for God. Do you, your family, and your church live this kind of faith in action?

Chaplain Kitchen was in the Persian Gulf to tend to the spiritual needs of his men, and he was able to do so because he had first earned their respect. The conversions and rededications among his men were many and sincere: these soldiers would still be living in the faith after the battles were over.

Like the sailors who turned to Chaplain Kitchen, President Bush called on Reverend Billy Graham. Like the chaplain, Reverend Graham had worked and labored hard. He had set examples and taken the high road in life. He had listened to God and he had talked directly to men and women—not preached down to them. When our nation needed God, it was only natural that our President would call on Reverend Graham, a proven man of God.

Both of these men—one in the military and practically unknown and the other the most famous preacher of our day—were responsible for influencing lives and saving souls during Desert Storm. They did so by living a life with which no one could find fault. If all Christians lived that way, then revival wouldn't be necessary—our whole nation would already know the Lord! In God's mysterious ways, the actions of a few can encourage many to follow—and people were following. Reverend Graham and Chaplain Kitchen were working mightily for the Lord. And these two weren't alone.

More than one hundred of our Full Gospel chaplains were also leading by example. Like Klon, they were not reaching souls simply by preaching. They were reaching the troops because of what the soldiers saw in their lives. Our chaplains were born-again, faithful, and compassionate men and women. In response to their calling, they were working hard for the Lord and reaching out to everyone around them. Rather than complaining about the insanity of Saddam or the futility of war, they were seeing the war as an opportunity to do the Lord's work. A lost soldier who saw this couldn't help but be moved.

Many times, soldiers have told their chaplains that they never believed in Jesus until they saw Him in another Christian's eyes. Because we had so many hardworking, believing Christians—both as chaplains and among the troops—and because so many people on the home front were writing, praying, and sending Bibles to the Gulf, frightened soldiers were, for the first time, seeing Jesus in a believer's eyes and actions. It's a shame we didn't have this fire for sharing the news of Christ all along, but at least when we realized how fragile life is and that war is not a thing of the past, we seized the power of the Gospel once again.

Soon after the air war began, Chaplain Michael Brown wrote a letter to my wife, part of which I share here:

> The reality of the war situation never hit home until we started receiving our gas masks. Even then, the seriousness was not felt by some. But as soon as we had our first real alert, you could finally sense the fear, finally feel the threat of war and the possibility of real battle and even death.

Death was on our doorstep. You could tell the difference between the sailors whose hope is in Christ and the ones who have no hope at all.

I have met many Christians since I've been in the Red Sea. Many are working hard for the Lord, reaping the harvest of this present age. But it breaks my heart to see those who are asleep on the job. A few are leading lives contrary to God's Word. They aren't living a life that reflects Christ, and they're certainly not providing counsel or support for the men and women on their ships.

We work anywhere from fifteen to twenty-one hours a day, and our schedule shows no date for us to return home. In the beginning, I wondered why God would send me into a war. Now I know. God's people have always been at war. He only placed me on a different battlefield. I thank Him for the many souls who are coming to know Him as Lord and Savior.

Michael's words should touch the soul of every lazy Christian. What good is there in hiding your lamp? If our chaplains had followed the strict wishes of the Saudi government, there would have been no light in the Middle East. Yet our chaplains didn't hide. They took chances and reached out. God protected them, and a revival began. Yet, in our own land, a place where the practice of religion is a matter of free choice, we often hide our spirit and fail to reach out with God's love to those who need us.

Miracles are waiting for those who believe in God. Thousands of men who had killed, raped, looted, and sold drugs in the United States, were saved in Saudi because a chaplain made the effort to invite them to a service. The chaplain didn't shake his head and say, "I wish I could reach that soldier." Instead he reached out because he knew that God was with him and would help him in his mission. Most of the lost aren't lost because they enjoy a life of pain, misery, and darkness. They are lost because they have never had a joyful, Spirit-filled Christian show them what being filled with the Spirit is really all about.

Beverly, one of our Gulf chaplains, certainly had a way of reaching out and sharing the light. Although she worked all day leading Bible studies and spending hours with those who requested one-on-one sessions, she would still find time to distribute Bibles, tapes, and Christian bookmarks. If she discovered a lost soul who didn't want a Bible but needed a toothbrush, she found that for him. She would help in whatever way she could—and a lot of those who at first wanted only a toothbrush later came back for a Bible and then for salvation.

She wrote to us:

> Did three services yesterday—one with a baptism—and, during the third, there was a RED ALERT in the middle of the message. We took cover until it was over, and then everyone came back and stayed until the end. . . I am now reaching four hundred in services, and the message I am teaching has been a big hit. Two more were baptized last Sunday in an outboard motor cleaning tank. Our engineers set it up.

You know "Semper Fidelis" is the Marine

Corps motto. It means "always faithful," and it seems especially fitting for the work which is ours here and also for those at home who support us. Your faith has certainly uplifted me.

"Always faithful" does indeed seem to describe our chaplains during Desert Storm. While many of us were glued to CNN, the chaplains were too busy sharing the story of Jesus to worry about what might happen when the ground war began. Projections about the number of casualties would only remind them of what they already knew too well—that the significant losses were those who died not knowing Jesus. So our people did their best to make sure that everyone they met had heard the Good News about our Lord.

Our people modeled a life of faith in a variety of ways. Chaplain Arley Longworth, for instance, knew that he had a job to do, but when he went to the doctor to have a reoccurring pain checked, X-rays revealed a huge gallstone. There was no choice but to operate, a procedure which would knock him out of service for a long time. He told the doctors he could not leave his troops until after Christmas. They needed him. In the meantime, he would pray for healing. The doctors shook their heads and told him these things just don't go away. He returned to his unit and sought the Lord's healing touch. When he checked in for surgery, the doctors couldn't remove the gallstone—because it wasn't there! It had dissolved. Even the physicians admitted that this had to be a miracle.

As a smiling Arley went back to work, Aubrey Jackson wrote us about how excited he was that the war was actually beginning. He saw this as a mighty opportunity for the Lord to work in Saudi:

> Yes, it's war! It's been that way for a long time. But when the smoke clears, the body of Christ will be standing—in Saudi Arabia, in Europe, in America, and around the world—with sin, the flesh, and the Devil under our feet!
>
> I'm proud to be a small part of God's great army!

Klon Kitchen added:

> My dear mother once told me that "man can't put you where God can't use you." And I truly believe that now. . . On this cruise, we have had several people find the Lord Jesus for the first time, and we've seen many rededications. The Spirit of the Lord is ever with us.

Rather than ask to be somewhere else, our men and women thanked God for the opportunities that came with their assignment in the Gulf. They hadn't wanted war; they had prayed for peace. But when war came, they decided that "Desert Storm" would be the name of the hurricane of soul-winning that could be done if they were willing to work.

From the *USS Worden*, Duane Purser wrote:

> Programs on the ship are great! Attendance is way up, and guys that I never expected to see give their lives to the Lord are turning to Him in faith. This slimline [Bible] is a great tool. The men love

to put it in their pocket and read the Word when they get a chance. . . Lots of men have asked for Bibles. I have already given away the hundred you sent me. . . I am having a wonderful time of ministry!

As battles raged, services were heavily attended, and at least one person gave his or her life to the Lord at every meeting. Our people reported that these were not "foxhole conversions," but rather sincere commitments to God and the Christian lifestyle. Soldiers just didn't give in and say, "Okay, I'd better protect my soul just in case." Rather, they came running up to the altar, tears rolling down their faces, to ask the Lord into their hearts. These were not just booster shots—they were lifetime inoculations!

Chaplains were now telling us that services were so well attended that there wasn't room for all who wanted to get in. Men were coming early, saving seats, and even begging their COs for a larger meeting place. Usually the COs complied because they wanted to attend the service too!

Two weeks ago, eighty men came to worship and praise Christ. Men are accepting Christ in the Bible study and at church services. Praise the Lord! Too bad it takes a war to get men thinking about eternity, but they're thinking now—and God is using this to His advantage!—Lieutenant David K. Sanders, *USS Denver*

With the outbreak of the war, many men have had serious questions concerning their faith. This is the most open I have ever seen this crew. Men are starving and hungry for the Word of God! PTL! Approximately twenty men have committed their lives to the Lord in the last eighteen days of fighting. On this ship, that is a major revival! The crew usually gets less than five hours of sleep a day, and—in spite of the stress that comes with the constant threat of mines and enemy aircraft and surface vessels—these guys still find time to worship and attend Bible study, prayer meetings, and regular services. We are at an all-time high!—Duane Purser, *USS Worden*

A great many of our chaplains also wrote letters triumphantly proclaiming their new religious freedom in Saudi. The government restrictions on worship had been rescinded. Crosses could now be displayed, people could pray in public, and the Gospel could come out into the open in the Middle East! Chaplains were now officially chaplains, not merely morale officers.

Meanwhile, as more and more men and women on the front lines came to know the Lord and we were truly winning an unparalleled victory for Christ, our air power was finding the war against Iraq very one-sided. Saddam and his fighting machine seemed to be holding its ground, waiting for something and offering little more than token resistance. Iraq was firing Scud missiles, but they were armed with limited warheads and not chemical weapons. Furthermore, these attacks seemed to be aimed more at Israel's civilian population than our troops. Saddam was apparently trying to drag the Israelis into the war in hopes of splitting the Arab alliance against him. He must have figured that his Islamic neighbors would rather fight with him than be on the side of the Jews. As it turned out, the United States convinced Israel to allow us to handle Saddam by bringing in our forces to intercept the Scuds. So the Arab alliance held firm.

With the war going so well—as one reporter put it, with "the storm blowing in one direction"—we wondered just what Saddam had up his sleeve. He had promised to fight us to the death, but he was grounding his planes in Iran, his best troops hid in bunkers, and he failed to attack. He simply stayed put.

The only time we were reminded of Saddam's wicked ways was when he put captured American and allied pilots on television, but even this attempt to weaken our resolve failed. Watching our men read prepared statements just made us more ready to end this dictator's demonic rule.

Even though few people had suggested it, Saddam's evil nature may have helped the Christian cause among our troops. In their minds, they were fighting a flesh-and-blood devil. As a result, they found themselves even more fearful of the real Satan. Saddam would pale in comparison to the Angel of Evil, and this seemed to waken a number of people to the condition of their own lives.

Our chaplains reported that many soldiers came

to them saying, "My life is worth nothing. I have never been any good. In fact, I'm scarcely better than the guy we're fighting." Those who had taken such a close look at their own dismal lives were more than ready to embrace Christ, His love, and His ways. They might never have been forced to face themselves and their sins if they hadn't looked into the guns of the evil Saddam.

While we waited to see when the ground war would start, most of us kept praying mightily. We acknowledged that God had given us grand protection in the air, but we wondered what would happen when we faced the bloodthirsty Iraqis on the ground. We feared that many would die. After all, we had never fought an enemy like this one.

As we waited and wondered, our now-desperate enemy began pouring millions of barrels of oil into the Gulf and setting afire those oil wells on land. Even though we didn't know it at the time, the Iraqis were also stealing medical supplies and electronic equipment and executing any man, woman, or child who appeared to be helping the Kuwaiti resistance. Throughout Kuwait, smoke and death hung in the air as that country's people waited for the allied forces to move in and challenge the invaders.

The wait was a long one. The war began on January 16 with the first of tens of thousands of air strikes. We didn't invade on the ground until February 23. A proverb of the Islamic religion says, "He who eats his fill while his neighbors go without food is not a believer." What we saw when we entered Kuwait and met the Iraqi Army is that Saddam is hardly a follower of Islam. While he had lived comfortably and eaten well in his bunker, safe from Allied attacks and bombing raids, his men had taken the assault head-on. Haunted by endless air strikes on their positions, Saddam's troops had been given no hope or guidance, and they had literally been starved to death. Their leader may have been enjoying the meat of a fatted calf, but he asked them to make do on a cup of rice a day.

As our soldiers moved in, the Iraqis moved forward to greet us—not in anger or a warlike stance but rather with hands lifted in surrender. Hungry, tired, and completely demoralized, they not only turned themselves in, but they gave their weapons to unarmed chaplains and members of the news media. They asked to be captured.

In the first twenty-four hours of battle—if you could call it that—more than thirty thousand Iraqis gave up. They had been praying for the United States to invade so that they would have a chance to live. They wanted nothing more of allied firepower, Kuwait, or Saddam.

Suddenly, the tens of thousands of the American soldiers who had given themselves over to the Lord in the months and days before battle were witnessing the miracle they had prayed for—the war was almost bloodless. We had stood up for right and been a leader in a moral cause, and our enemy had backed down with very little fight. No one had expected it, no one had even really hoped for it, but it had happened. Why? Had God heard our prayers?

Had He been moved when a nation, its leadership, and its fighting men and women fell to their knees and cried out to Him? The Bible is filled with such miracles.

Consider this fact, too: More than anything else, we were concerned that Saddam would use poison gas. When he was given the January 15 deadline, we felt he might wait until January or February to try it. Whenever he did resort to using gas, we knew that many men and women would die, no matter how thorough our precautions. Yet the attack never came. The reason? The winds which always blow from the northwest at that time of year were miraculously always blowing from the south this year. If the poison gas had been released, the only people who would have died would have been Iraq's troops. So Saddam's only real weapon—the only weapon which offered massive destructive power—was knocked out by an unusual change in wind direction—the wind that is under God's control.

As Day One of the ground war ended and Day Two began, men and women on the battlefront were falling to their knees in thankfulness. As freed Kuwaitis hugged them, the soldiers responded by thanking their Lord for the ease of victory. In the midst of Desert Storm, He had brought peace to both the land and to the soul. The war would soon be over, but the effects of what had happened spiritually were just beginning to appear. Chaplain Wayne Harris telephoned after the Ground Battle, via his mother to us in Dallas. Prior to the battle they held a special service of dedication and commitment. Wayne spoke forth a Word from God, that the air war had not lasted but 40 days (a Biblical number) and the ground war could not last seven days. This was difficult to believe, as everyone expected several weeks. It was over in 100 hours, as we now all know. Upon the troops returning to base camp, following the battle, they held a three hour praise and worship service.

Chaplain L.J. DiIulio shares an experience that seems to have happened again and again throughout the Gulf. God came to him and touched him in a way he could never before have imagined. He knew that he would leave the Gulf a different man—not for just a few months or years, but forever. Listen to his story:

> The real blessing I've received in the midst of all this war and talk of war is taking place in my own heart. The Lord is doing a deep and wonderful work in my life.
>
> Like Jacob, I have been having my own Bethel experience here in Saudi. As you recall the story of Jacob, his flight from his brother Esau took him to a place called Bethel, the house of God. It was there that he met the Lord and built his altar. His altar was significant because it was the only place on which Jacob could sacrifice anything unto the Lord and leave it with Him. At Bethel, things which kept Jacob separated from God but that he had kept hidden in his heart were revealed. You see, it was at the altar in Bethel that Jacob drew closer to the Lord through his acts of sacrifice and prayer.
>
> Like Jacob, I have come to my Bethel here in

Saudi, and I have built my own altar. And as I lie before my altar, those things which need to be purged from my heart are revealed. I find myself falling more and more deeply in love with my Savior Jesus. It has not been so much an act of seeking; it's been more an act of the Lord's invitation.

My Bethel experience continues to be one of sanctification. I don't believe we should ever feel as though we've arrived in our ministry. I've just begun to taste the deep riches of Christ in my fellowship with Him. The process of sanctification is a continual pattern of growth during which His disciples fall more and more in love with the Master.

Like Jacob, I've been led of the Lord to build an altar here in Saudi. The Lord is doing a deep work in me and blessing me as I fellowship with Him at my altar.

I believe the Lord has called all of us to be altar-builders. My desire and prayer is that all of us who are a part of the Chaplaincy of Full Gospel Churches become altar-builders in our own Bethel.

I am blessed to have been able to serve with you in the Lord's army.

The war had really just begun, but it was almost over. Christians had taken up the "shield" of the Lord and "stormed" His truth into the desert. Now they were almost ready to bring this victory in the name of Jesus home. It had almost been a sacrifice without loss.

Then, in the dark of night on February 25, as the multinational force continued to take back Kuwait in a sweep too impossibly easy for anyone to have predicted, Saddam made one last desperate move. Earlier in the day, he had gone on radio and commanded his soldiers to "kill with all your might." He tried one more time to portray the American forces as enemies of God. Even as he spoke, his men were either giving up by the tens of thousands or running as fast as they could to try to beat the American assault to the border. Seeing his military might crumble, Saddam ordered another Scud attack. This time he aimed it at an American base in Al Khobar, Saudi Arabia.

The missile tore into an American barracks, exploding as men and women slept—perhaps dreaming of an easy victory and an early reunion with loved ones. Henry Young, one of our own chaplains, was there. The next day he called and told me what he had seen.

He reported that the building had been almost completely destroyed and that bodies were all over the place. Men and women were crying, calling out for help and for news about others in the building. Of those who weren't killed, many were very badly injured. For the first time, it really looked to these Americans as if the war had hit our side, too.

As Henry reached out to hold hands and pray, he noted other Americans—those who had escaped injury—doing the same. As crews worked to find victims and take the wounded to hospitals, prayer seemed to be what those waiting for transport wanted most—and what those who had come alongside were doing with a passion.

Chaplains of all denominations were at the site

within minutes. Together with doctors and nurses, these men of God were attempting to answer questions, calm anxious hearts, and reach deep down into dying men's souls. At this horrific scene of war—in front of the Saudis, the press, and the television cameras—these Christian servants were openly doing the Master's bidding.

When it was all over and the body count completed, twenty-eight Americans had been killed and another ninety wounded in Saddam's final offensive, terroristic thrust. It was a terrible waste of life, and yet it sharply reminded all of us just how bloody this war could have been. After all, Iraq had the numbers, they had billions of dollars in military equipment, and they had had the time to dig in—yet they hadn't fought. Scarcely twenty-four hours after the Scud hit our barracks, Iraq surrendered.

The number of American deaths directly attributed to fighting in the Persian Gulf War was only seventy-nine. Just under eighty men and women died in a war to which we had deployed over five hundred thousand. Another 213 soldiers were wounded. There is little doubt that more may be injured and possibly even die during cleanup operations, but a death rate of .0158 percent is a miracle.

The number of Americans killed in Gulf War combat during the whole course of operations—in excess of six months—was fewer than the average number of people killed each day in alcohol-related automobile accidents in the United States. Our troops were actually safer in Saudi, on the seas, and invading Kuwait and Iraq than they would have been at home. This is a miracle of prayer. And may this miracle—God's preservation of the gift of life and His safekeeping of so many soldiers—lay the foundation for a revival that will touch every man, woman, and child in our country and beyond.

CHAPTER 10

A Storm of Revival

"If God ever took sides in a war, He was on our side in this one. We had two killed in action and thirty-six wounded. We have over three thousand Iraqi prisoners right now. I don't know how many Iraqis were killed. Seven thousand to ten thousand, if I had to make a wild guess."

General Ronald Griffith—U.S. 1st Armored Division

IN THE FINAL DAYS OF THE WAR, A FACT BECAME OBVIous to those on the front lines as well as to those watching the action on television. The men we were taking as POWs were receiving better treatment from us than they were from their own army.

In World War II, we treated prisoners so well that many felt a special warmth and respect for America and its people. Many German POWs made trips back to the United States in order to visit those who had held them captive. They often brought their children and grandchildren to see the places where they had been held. During these visits, hardships were not mentioned. Instead, dinner conversations again and again focused on the kindness shown them by the "enemy," the American forces.

American soldiers who were taken as POWs in

World War II did not receive such treatment in the Axis camps. Their memories of being held captive by the Germans, the Japanese, and the Italians were far from good. They didn't yearn to relive old times or meet the enemy with a handshake and a smile. Their images of being captured were colored by hatred and mistrust.

The spirit of America—the compassion, the respect for human life, and the willingness to care for the hurting—makes us unique in the world. Although we have fallen far away from our Founding Fathers' religious precepts, we have still reached out with a gentle hand to those who have been forced to surrender to us. In the Persian Gulf War, for instance, we not only fed our enemy, but we gave them first-class medical treatment, new clothes, and warm beds. Even knowing that Iraq was mistreating our men and women didn't make us sink to their level. Don't you think that the way we treated the Iraqi prisoners will have a lasting effect on them? Doesn't our treatment of prisoners open the door of the Muslim world for Christ? Doesn't everyone want to be loved by and to serve a God who loves them?

We may never know the long-term spiritual results of our care for the Iraqi prisoners, but we do know about the many American service men and women who received God's love and Jesus Christ as their Savior while they were serving overseas. Before we discuss the impact these new believers will have on a Christian revival in our own land, we need to realize what is already going on around the world.

We are living in a time when Christians face unprecedented evangelistic opportunities. The 1990s can be a time of spiritual harvest like we have never known before!

Right now, thirty-five hundred new churches are opening around the world every day—not in a year, but each and every day! The church in China, an atheistic nation that remains repressive and hostile to outside influence, is gaining over twenty-eight thousand new converts each day. The number of Christians in this most backward of the communist superpowers is already between twenty-five and fifty million.

In Africa each day, about twenty thousand people convert from either the Muslim religion or tribal worship to life-giving faith in Jesus. That part of the continent below the Sahara is already forty percent Christian. In southeast Asia, one-quarter of the population of Indonesia, a strictly Islamic nation, is Christian even though the worship of Jesus is strongly discouraged. And with the opening of Eastern Europe, we have heard much encouraging news about people hearing and embracing the Gospel of Jesus Christ. Never has the world been so ripe for the Lord, and never have we His people been so ready to act.

It is predicted that by the year 2000, every "people" group in the world will have heard about Jesus. Various evangelizing denominations (including the Southern Baptists, Assemblies of God, and others) have the framework for this mission already in place. This missionary movement, however, extends beyond the U.S. borders. The people of Korea, for instance, a country that didn't even allow Christianity until earlier in this century, are rapidly being converted by Korean missionaries who are reaching out to their own people.

In the U.S.S.R., there is not only a growing interest in Christianity among the common people, but among the elite as well. Scholars and government leaders are studying the Word of God. They are also actively encouraging evangelism. Leaders in the highest positions are calling upon God for help in rebuilding their nation. Even Communist Party members are studying how to bring Christianity into their party's platform.

So what are the major obstacles to saving the world? What is there to keep us from claiming mankind for Christ? Until recently, the major barrier was said to be the hold of Islam and Hinduism, but with the results of the Gulf War, this analysis may no longer be accurate. The world situation may be changing, and that change may be quite dramatic.

George Otis, president of the Seattle-based Sentinel Group, reported at InterVarsity Christian Fellowship's "Urbana '90" missions conference that ". . . extraordinary things are happening in the [Islamic] region that defy normal methods of evangelism. Although few missionaries work in Muslim-dominated countries, God is clearly moving among truth-seeking Muslims through power encounters, healings, and other supernatural occurrences. These things expedite conversions." He reports numerous such events in Algeria, Tunisia,

Morocco, Turkey, Saudi Arabia, Iran, and Soviet Central Asia. Christ is opening a door for us in areas that we thought were impossible to enter; He is providing exciting opportunities to spread the message of Jesus' love and salvation.

With our own president so openly embracing prayer and the power of God, America once again seems proud to stand up and be counted as a God-fearing nation. And this hasn't been the case since the days just after World War II. Once again we seem ready to be the "God, apple pie, and mom" nation that was once a moral influence for the whole world.

Even with these wonderful opportunities for evangelism at hand, with statistics reporting more and more people worldwide becoming followers of Jesus Christ, and with church attendance and prayer in the U.S. at a new high, can we be sure that our world is really ready for a change? Can we be sure that we in the United States are capable of leading that change? Can we point to one sign indicating that Americans are ready to lead the way in doing God's will and directing millions of people to Christ over the next decade?

I personally think the signs are there. First, there are the tens of thousands of young men and women who discovered Christ during the days of Desert Shield and Desert Storm. Second, there is the mood of the world and the atmosphere here at home. I have seen this mood before, this openness to God and enthusiasm for His work. Now, seeing this mood coupled with the unbelievable Christian spirit that embraced our men and women in the

Gulf, I have to believe that we are on the brink of an evangelical miracle the likes of which none of us has ever known!

The end of Persian Gulf hostilities marked the beginning of a huge homecoming celebration. Depending on what happens in the Gulf, this homecoming may be played out over the next six months. Reunion after reunion will make us laugh and cry and feel good about ourselves, our country, and our military men and women. Still, we must remember what these men and women have come through. We must consider what they have experienced—the terror of war, the pain of separation, the stress of living with the unknowns of battle, the contact with a very different culture—and realize that these things will have changed them forever.

I know firsthand how stressful war can be. When people are living with severe and constant stress, they turn to something or someone outside of themselves for relief. Where they turn often determines not only their future, but it can also affect the future of those people around them. When a whole segment of society turns to one thing, that movement can dramatically change the perspective and goals of an entire nation.

World War II was a war in which most Americans could participate with a clear conscience. We knew that the war had to be fought for freedom in our own land as well as for freedom around the world. Because of this understanding, there was a national unity like we had never before witnessed. Morale was high in both the military and civilian sectors. It was a time when God could work in the hearts and lives of people. Following our victory over the Axis powers, a great many people turned—and re-turned—to the Lord. Americans went to school, to college, to Bible classes, and to seminaries in order to deepen their understanding of the world, their Lord, and how He works in His people's lives. Many young servicemen and women sensed and answered a call of God.

During this period of time, churches grew rap-idly. The Southern Baptists, with their emphasis on evangelism and their construction of new semi-naries, really took off. They provided tremendous leadership in a new evangelical movement that was sweeping the nation. Other denominations, particu-larly the Pentecostals led by the Assemblies of God, took root and grew like never before. These groups found a ready audience for their Gospel message in both rural and urban America. The Good News was listened to, and it was believed. Those who had come back from war now wanted to understand why they had been spared. War had matured them. They had all been deeply affected by what they had expe-rienced, and they had come face-to-face with their own mortality. Now they saw the Lord as Someone they and their families needed. Most of all, they wanted a faith that was personal.

The denominations I mentioned have continued to grow since the end of World War II. They have grown because they have allowed God to reach men and women through them. They have served as ready and willing conduits of God's love and hope for a nation that wanted the Gospel.

The Church was not the only institution to be dramatically changed by the returning G.I.'s. While it was true that there was a temporary rash of divorces—due in large part to the long years of stress and separation—family life actually flourished once husbands and fathers returned home. These military men wanted to be a part of a family. Husbands and wives let themselves depend on one another; they spent time together and cherished that time; and they responded sensitively and willingly to each other's needs. Children were seen as vital and important, and time devoted to parenting became one of the most treasured of all commodities. The new wave of Christian growth meant God being present in homes, and as a result families became more stable and loving than they had ever been. God was moving in bright and wonderful ways, and because we had been so near losing all that we treasured, we were responding as individuals and as a nation in a deeply moral manner. The United States was proud but humble, a leader among nations, and the most respected country and people in the world.

At the beginning of the Persian Gulf War forty-five years later, however, the church and the family in America were very different. Most denominations in the United States were shrinking and dying, and long-held ideals for the American family were crumbling. We were no longer a moral leader, and we often found ourselves less-than-respected when it came to world affairs. While the Southern Baptists' records showed a large number of annual baptisms and the Assemblies of God and a few other Pentecostal groups were registering significant growth, no denomination had experienced a real "revival fever" in some time. And it was just too early to tell whether the new nondenominational Spirit-filled, charismatic, or Neo-Pentecostal believers—groups that seemed to be growing rapidly—could maintain their momentum.

After World War II, churches were strong and prepared to lead the wave of new Christians and moral growth. Now, forty-five years later, who is going to lead this new revival? Who will step forward? Will it be an established group? Will it be a new force? Will it be anyone at all?

The new and renewed believers who are returning from the deserts of Saudi and the ships of the Gulf—the harvest of souls reaped in the war—are coming home to a warm welcome. Psychologically, America is healthy. We can hold our heads high again, not embarrassed or confused as we were after Korea and especially Vietnam. The Vietnam War, undeclared yet financed by Congress and supported by the country's leadership, was the most divisive event to hit our country since the Civil War. It literally destroyed national unity, American morale, and the ideal of pulling together for a common goal. We became a fragmented and cynical people. The days and months after the war did not offer a good environment for preaching or spreading the Gospel.

As badly as we were doing as a people, our Vietnam veterans were the ones who really suffered.

Most of them had been drafted to serve in a situation they didn't understand, told to do things that made little sense, and used for a war that had no meaning or conclusion. Since our participation in that conflict ended, more Vietnam veterans have died as a result of suicide—more than sixty thousand individuals—than died in actual battle. The scars of the war ran deep, and the experience caused Americans to lose faith when it was most needed. As Christians, we didn't offer the right kind of leadership on a large enough scale, and a whole generation turned away from the church and embraced other means of finding peace. Usually what these seekers found was just more pain and emptiness.

But now, in the aftermath of the Persian Gulf War, there is a unity reminiscent of the days after World War II, and the Lord Jesus places a great premium on such unity. Matthew 18:19 says, "If two of you shall agree on earth as touching any thing that they shall ask, it shall be done for them of my Father which is in heaven." Notice that this Scripture doesn't speak of faith as a requirement for God's response; the focus is on making an agreement or uniting. And in 1991, we are again a United States.

In Vietnam our young men were just that— young men. The average age was just twenty years. In the Persian Gulf War, our men and women averaged twenty-seven years. During this seven-year period, a young person matures significantly. Our service personnel were therefore better prepared for the experiences in the desert than their counterparts were for the jungles of Vietnam. And what our soldiers found in Saudi will spur and enhance their personal growth rather than stagnate it. They will be able to use what they have seen and learned as soon as they get home and again and again for the rest of their lives.

Also, as I mentioned earlier, the war in Saudi was a sober war. Drugs and alcohol were strictly forbidden. Our soldiers, then, were clearheaded and very aware of their surroundings and the lessons about life that were waiting to be learned. So, besides being older and more mature, our soldiers' sobriety enabled them to benefit from what they experienced.

Another important fact to remember is that this was a war fought by married people. A greater percentage of our fighting force was married than at any other time in our country's history. And even though they usually served in different units, many husband-and-wife couples were stationed in the Gulf at the same time. Back home, thanks to television and tremendous media coverage, the families of these men and women could keep track of what was happening to their loved ones. They could call toll-free numbers for daily news updates. They could immediately check casualty lists and stay in phone contact with people who knew the soldiers about whom they were most concerned.

This war had a closeness, a degree of reality and intensity, that we on the home front had never before known. The media provided us all with an immediate window to what was going on. Because we "were there," we can now better relate to the service men and women as they come home. This understanding on our part should allow us as a nation to draw even closer together. Also, although spouses missed their mates, they could stay in touch virtually around the clock thanks to today's electronics and satellite communications. Husbands and wives may not find themselves having to bridge a huge gap created by the time spent apart: an at-home wife who watched TV and read newspapers knows a lot about the world her soldier husband experienced.

Finally, and most importantly, these men and women are coming home to a country that was "one nation, under God," more united now than at any other time in recent history. Again and again, our president, members of Congress, and many of our top military brass called on the name of God and asked us to pray with them. This type of faith in action may have actually begun in families and small churches, eventually touching our national leaders. After all, thousands of churches created prayer chains and held special prayer meetings just for the Gulf War situation. Many thousands of Americans wrote letters and sent Bibles and crosses to the soldiers overseas. Countless backsliders came back to the fold. Initially, this massive grass-roots movement may have influenced the spiritual leadership of our nation, and later that leadership no doubt influenced thousands of other churches and millions of other Christians in their faith. We were encouraging one another to pray to God during the stressful days of Desert Shield and Desert Storm.

This turning to God through prayer was so amazing—politicians, members of the armed forces, and men and women from all walks of life were openly seeking God—that even the secular press noted it. We at home also seemed, at least for a few months, to disregard the erroneous concept of the separation of church and state. We seemed to ignore the agnostic or atheistic element of our society that has brought to an end so many religious activities that were once important markers of our nation's Christian heritage. In our time of common need, we called upon the one true Leader of all people for His help.

And the massive cry of Americans on both sides of the world uniting in prayer was heard by the Lord. The windows of heaven were thrown open, and God's salvation, His grace, and His mercy poured forth.

Will we now go forward with God? Will we focus on what is important, on what we have in common as believers rather than our unique differences? Will we let God, through His Son Jesus and the blessed Holy Spirit, move in His church in America? Will we let God act in His own perfect time in the 1990s? Will we see our nation awakened spiritually, revived and restored? And what if God moves in a way different from what our denomination or our personal experience suggests—will we attempt to move with Him? Or will we balk and demand that He increase the family of believers our way?

These questions are important as we consider the kind of revival we will see over the next ten years. Many a human endeavor has had a promising beginning but has never been completed. What we do now will determine much of this nation's and Christianity's future in the world.

God moved sovereignly in the desert, and thousands of people were blessed. Pray that we will rejoice when He moves here at home and America is blessed. Let none say that God can't do it. And let us together believe in His blessing for the whole world—a world which includes the Muslim nations and the enemy we just defeated.

Every survey and poll certifies that we Americans believe in God and in the hereafter. Right now, more of us believe in heaven and hell than at any other recent time. The American people are ready.

In 1991, the American population is very much aware of the term "born again." Thanks to President Jimmy Carter, this term is not new to many people. Many folks may not know exactly what it means, but they have heard the phrase.

The general population is also familiar with the terms "Spirit-filled" and "Full Gospel." Perhaps this is due to those businessmen who always "meet to eat," or to the television evangelists who have preached so loudly, taken in so much money, and then, in some well-publicized cases, misused it. Still, the terms are no longer foreign to the American population.

Obviously, God has seen to it that we in America are aware of certain religious and spiritual terms. Some of us only need to have an accurate definition put to these phrases. We don't need legalistic, denominational tradition; we need the pure and simple Word of God. After all, the Word tells us the Spirit makes alive, but the law kills.

Half a million young Americans are coming home, and their world will never be like it was prior to August 1990. While they were stationed in the Gulf, many of them had a personal encounter with the living God through His Son Jesus and the Holy Spirit. They came to know Him outside of church walls under the canopy of an Arabian sky in the same land were Christ once preached and taught in the open fields. These new believers now know that they can count on God—a marvelous, miracle-working God—even if they can't count on much else.

These young men and women will want to live for Jesus and walk in daily fellowship with God. They won't want to be boxed into some denominational bureaucrat's system. They will want to know more about the God of the Bible. Many will know a "call of God" upon their lives, and they will want help in preparing for their complete response to that call as they go forth in God's world.

The men and women who served in the reserves and the National Guard are also returning from service in the Gulf War. They will come home to the same towns and cities, the same homes and offices, which they left. They will return to the same jobs—but they will be different. They will carry with them the seeds of revival, and they will be looking for a way to plant and nurture those seeds.

The men and women returning to America will be welcomed home in style. Many of our cities have enlarged this celebration to include those service personnel who were never welcomed back from Vietnam. These veterans will lift heads and hearts as heroes, and deep wounds will begin to heal.

Those Americans who will welcome back the soldiers from the Gulf are the same people who prayed for them, wrote to them, and sent them gifts. They are the ones who hoped that each of these men and women would find the Lord and invite Him into their lives. They were the ones who planted the seeds that bore fruit during the days of war.

So the climate in America—as well as around the world—seems conducive for revival. We in the United States are ready to once again embrace a loving God.

We have proven in the Gulf War against Saddam that the United States has the power to defeat any enemy. We have the weapons, the technology, the mind power, the men and women, the resolve, and the faith in God to once again lead the world in a way that cannot be challenged. The question, then, for all Christians in America is, "Can we do the same in spiritual warfare?"

God has given us the weapons—His Word, the power of Jesus Christ and the Holy Spirit, the men and women who were saved in the Gulf—but do we have the resolve? The fields are rich and fertile, the climate has never been better, miracles have already happened, the Lord has shown that He will work through us, and our own people have shown that they are ready to hear and accept His word in faith. So will we finish what has begun in the Gulf? Will we join with God in creating a new wave of world-wide enthusiasm for His Word?

The Lord God has always wanted to bless and not curse. It is His very nature to be kind and gentle, and He is the one who has set the stage for this, the greatest era of blessing in America's history. Will we believe it and will we receive it?

You are invited, as is your family and church, to be a part of this wonderful revival. Pray and let the living God direct you to your place of witness and service in His kingdom on earth. Help us spread throughout the world the Christian revival that has begun because of the Gulf War. Let us not let the spirit of revival fade until we have reached everyone for Christ! We have the tools, everything is in place, the mission has been set forth, and people are asking for our help. We have the message: "For God so loved the *world*, that he gave his only begotten Son, that whosoever believeth in him shall not perish, but have eternal life." (John 3:16) It is now up to us to actively share that message.

Saddam dared us as a nation to stop him—and we did. The Devil is now daring Christians to take back a world that he has unlawfully stolen. The world is crying for revival. Will we respond with the same kind of leadership, determination, and spirit that we did in the Gulf? Are we ready to play our part in a revival that will storm the world with Christ's love? A world that is hungry for the saving power of Jesus Christ is waiting for the Church's response.

About the Authors

CHAPLAIN E. H. JIM AND CHARLENE AMMERMAN ARE director and deputy director of the Chaplaincy of Full Gospel Churches, an agency which has received Pentagon endorsement for its support role with America's Armed Forces.

Jim retired from the U.S. Army in 1977 as a colonel. He had served as a chaplain for twenty-three years. During his military career, Jim was assigned to the 82nd Airborne Division of paratroopers, the 101st Airborne Division (then under General William Westmoreland's command), the Green Berets, the 1st Cavalry Division, and the 1st Armored Division.

Jim's last European assignment was with the "V" Corps in Frankfurt, Germany, where he supervised the eighty-three chaplains from fourteen denominations who were offering spiritual support to fifty thousand troops plus their dependents. Immediately prior to his retirement, Jim served at Fort Leavenworth, Kansas. There he was post chaplain and pastor to the Command and General Staff College where one thousand of the Army's most promising mid-career officers train to be colonels and generals.

Born in Conway, Missouri, on July 20, 1925, Jim is a graduate of Baptist colleges and seminaries. Spirit-filled in 1938, he has been an ordained minister since 1946. He holds both Doctor of Theology and Doctor of Divinity degrees.

Rev. Charlene Ammerman, D.D., many years a military wife, served as protocol officer for the U.S. Army's largest Officers' Wives Club. She has attended management skills seminars and Christian leadership conferences and worked closely with her husband in missionary training schools.

Charlene has Spirit-given gifts of her own in the areas of discernment, counsel, speaking, and ministering. She has been before audiences and on television in America, New Zealand, Australia, Korea, the Philippines, and Europe.

Together, the Ammermans are spiritual parents for more than 150 military, prison, and hospital chaplains and lay workers, twenty-eight of whom served in Operation Desert Storm in 1990-1991.

Jim and Charlene were married in 1945 and are the parents of two sons and two daughters.

isang mid-career officers train to be color
generals.